FRAGMENTS OF A SHATTERED SOUL

MADE WHOLE

a memoir

Love Lyn

LYN E. AYRE

 FriesenPress

Suite 300 - 990 Fort St
Victoria, BC, V8V 3K2
Canada

www.friesenpress.com

The author has written, over her lifetime, all of the poetry, prayers, essays, and short stories appearing in this book.

Lyn E. Ayre created the cover graphic using acrylic paints.

No part of this book should be used in lieu of sound medical advice from a licensed physician.

"This is a personal memoir of my own experience and opinions. It is my hope that this volume will bring comfort and joy to all seekers of solutions, faith, love, and peace. Many of the names have been changed by request of my living relatives. My name remains as is."

ISBN
978-1-5255-3440-9 (Hardcover)
978-1-5255-3441-6 (Paperback)
978-1-5255-3442-3 (eBook)

1. MEMOIR, CHRONIC ILLNESS, ADDICTION, SPIRITUAL RECOVERY

Distributed to the trade by The Ingram Book Company

TABLE OF CONTENTS

PART ONE:
Fragments of a Shattered Soul

PART TWO:
Made Whole

REVIEWS

"This courageous story of personal and spiritual survival in the face of huge challenges is told in an intimate voice that holds nothing back from the reader. In places harrowing to read, it is difficult to put down." *Eileen Kernaghan, author of nine books including 'Sophie, in Shadow'*

This personal memoir spans the vast array of human emotions, as Lyn chronicles her life-long search for a deeper spiritual connection. Her story will resonate with those who long to find peace while faced with incredible challenges." *Pauline Neck, author of 'Removing the Sting' and 'Discovering the Goodness of God'*

"'Fragments of a Shattered Soul Made Whole' is a raw and honest memoir. Lyn Ayre walks her readers through her personal struggle with abuse, addiction, and health. This is one woman's journey of healing and overcoming her fear." *Farida Somjee, author of 'The Beggar's Dance'*

"A great read! The author relates the extraordinary and ordinary events of her life as if she is conversing with the reader. The result is uplifting. The message is that life is to be experienced on life's terms-both good and bad, happy and sad. Loved it!" *Constance Bygrave, PhD, Assistant Professor, Fairleigh Dickinson University*

"'Fragments of a Shattered Soul Made Whole' is a compelling memoir that is both heartbreaking and heartwarming. Lyn Ayre bravely shares about the traumatic experiences, which took her down a dark path, and the self-healing that saved her. This book not only helps the reader understand that they are not alone in whatever challenges they may be facing, but that they, too, can find a path to not only coping but healing and thriving. A powerful book that will give you strength."
Melanie Cossey, author of 'A Peculiar Curiosity'

DEDICATION

Norman Joseph Ayre,
the person whose life I had the privilege of sharing for twenty-nine years, one month, three weeks, and two days. We used to tease that we would love each other for 'forever plus a day'. Now I know how long 'forever' is.

Norm accepted this shattered soul, as is. Then he found the glue, handed it to me, and held the pieces while I stuck the edges back together. Thank you, Sweetheart, for loving me just as I am. I'll never forget you and the impact you had on my life.

FOREWORD

It is seldom in life that one is offered the chance to be an observer as well as a participant in the life of a Soul who has climbed more ladders and reached more heights than is usual or probable in one lifetime.

When Lyn first honoured us with a friendship that has enriched our lives, she was at the bottom of a ladder. She blessed us with the opportunity to do something significant for a fellow human being. Our life was very simple. We had little to offer materially, but we offered what we had. Besides a roof over her head, we had love and encouragement to give Lyn, and the realization that she was a special person.

Like a butterfly emerging from a cocoon, it was a miracle to watch her unfold her wings and flex them. Then, steadily, she lifted them and started to soar. She has been soaring ever since.

This book is a reflection of much of the path Lyn has taken. Echoing many of the thoughts and attitudes she has experienced along the way. It is a partial expression of the spiritual adventure of her life. It will be worth your while to share it with her.

Louise Campbell Silver, Educator
February 10, 1920 to September 27, 2001
Salmon Arm, BC

INTRODUCTION

" Fragments of a Shattered Soul Made Whole" is the story of my life to age fifty. The first part of the book is fragmented memories, sometimes jumbled, many times jarring, often heartbreaking, hilarious, and maddening. The second part is more flowing, inspiring, and uplifting.

After Mom died, I wanted to write, "The Book of Vi". I realized I didn't know enough about her to do that. Through writing my story, I tell hers. There is no real thread to follow to reconstruct my childhood, only many frayed and timeworn fragments. So, I will let LOVE weave the tale using strands of silver-gold. I will use all of the other resources available to me, including intuitive inspiration at the beginning of the chapter called, 'Silverglade', to piece it all together.

The purpose of writing all of this down is to clarify, first to myself and then to you, who it is that 'I' call 'me'. This story is not 'the truth, the whole truth, and nothing but the truth'. Some memories were left out in respect of those who are still living and blessedly unaware of certain aspects of my life. Some things I am not ready to write about. I cannot relate all of the incidents that have made up my life. These are most of the highlights and lowlights, for, even in a panoramic scene, the periphery can get lost in the translation.

There are so many times when I hear my siblings tell stories about how it was while we were growing up and I think, *What are they talking about*"? I'm convinced, now, that they think the same thing when I share my recollections. We each have our own perspective on the events that have shaped our lives because we are, each of us, vastly different people. Such is the nature of a family. We've had very different experiences in life including our childhood. This book is *my* view. It tells about *my* spiritual journey, which took me to the darkest places of myself and brought me out to stand "In the Light".

My name is Lyn. I am, at times, troubled with obsessive/compulsive disorder (OCD), post-traumatic stress disorder (PTSD), systemic lupus (SLE), anti-phospholipid disorder (AP), arthritis, diabetes, and trigeminal neuralgia (TN). I'm a regular bowl of alphabet soup. These, however, are only medical labels used to describe some of the physical challenges I have to meet on a daily basis. These words are a just a few of the fragments in the mosaic of me. But this is not who *I* am. This does not define the whole of me. Nor do I allow it to control my life.

A sense of humour and wonder about how it works has kept me curious enough to stay and see how it all turns out. Thanks for joining me on my path to peace. Blessed be.

Lyn Ayre, Coquitlam, British Columbia, 23February2002
2018 update

Over the last sixteen years, I have revised and revisited every word of this book multiple times. After self-publishing as a .pdf in 2002, many copies were sold and well-received. This gave me the energy to keep going.

The diagnosis of MS was dropped, and fibromyalgia, peripheral neuropathy, and spinal stenosis were added. But *I'm* still trucking along.

You'll notice that I put the words 'I' and 'me' in italics, at times. This is to differentiate between who I AM (at my spirit-level) and who it is that I call Lyn. This is a common practice. We've all heard ourselves say, "Well, that's what *I* would do!"

A few years ago, my darling husband, Norman, passed away after eight years, off and on, with two types cancer. It was pure torture to see him go through what he did. The last fifteen hours were the worst. He gasped for every breath, still fighting hard for us. All he wanted to do was stay with me, with his family. We were deeply in love for all of our twenty-nine years together. I was very lucky to have had an amazing life with this man—the best person I'd ever met. To honour him and all he did for me, I keep putting one foot in front of the other and living my best life. I've grieved hard and worked harder to get a hold of myself and go on without him. Though I still miss him terribly, I love my life today. I've found happiness and purpose in art, writing, and cooking. When Norm and I met, he said, "God who"? The last thing he said to me was, "So much love, Lynnie. I feel surrounded by so much love." He was going to be with his God—LOVE.

I have gathered around me a beautiful family of friends who love and support me and who I can love and support, keeping the goodness flowing through me.

I feel that my life is about three-quarters tragedy and one-quarter triumph. I'm always making progress and becoming better than the day before. I heartily celebrate those special days when the pain isn't too bad, and the food is really good. My friends and my cat make me laugh. I learn patience, humility, and acceptance from the days when I'm on the couch too ill to move. I keep going forward. I'm grateful I know how to cook in large pots so I can freeze some and still eat well on those bad days. My son has been a treasure to me, and we've grown closer than I ever thought possible. Change is inevitable. Life is good.

I hope this book speaks to your heart and helps you in some way. I always enjoy hearing from my readers.

lynayre@telus.net and

www.lynayre.com

"Scars only show us where we've been.
They do not dictate where we're going."

–David Rossi–

PART ONE:

FRAGMENTS OF A SHATTERED SOUL

THE PATCHWORK KID

My first vivid memory is of my sister Victoria, age two, standing on the top landing of the steep stairs to the basement. I feel terrified because she is so high up. I am yelling "No, No!" but to no avail. I can clearly see her falling head over heels down the steps; red curls alternately pointing skyward then hidden under her frail body.

I hear my dad's voice yelling at me, blaming me. I protest and tell my dad that I had said 'no-no' to Vicki. He doesn't believe me and spanks me anyway. Deeply hurt by the injustice of it all, I run crying to my room. On the way, I pass the hall mirror, and I'm shocked to see my ugly, contorted face. I stop howling immediately. So, at the age of three, I made a life-changing decision to never cry again. It was then I knew that I needed to learn how to control my emotions.

I was born Lyn MacKay at the Royal Columbian Hospital in New Westminster, BC. It was a hot day, July 8, 1951, and mom tells me that my arrival caused a lot of excitement. I was brought home to 472 Garrett Street, the same house that my dad had been born in back in 1929.

My parents were Jeremy MacKay and Veronica Harris. Family stories say my birth seemed to forge their bond even stronger than before. I was completely loved and appreciated, in the beginning. I thrived being surrounded by my parents, grandparents, great-grandparents, and all manner of aunts and uncles. Life for me started out great.

Mom met my dad in the summer of 1950 when she was seventeen. She'd finished school at Queen Elizabeth Senior High in Surrey and was working as a switchboard operator for the BC Telephone Company. Mom and some of her friends had decided to go to a dance.

My dad was the leader of the band that night and had told one of his sidemen that the next young single gal to walk through the door was going to become his wife. It turned out to be my mother. When I think of this now, he was really taking a big chance. No one suspected the sizzling love affair that was starting. They were married that year on December 29, 1950.

In my early years, Dad was a pivotal character in my life. He was very exacting in his ways pertaining to disciplining children and his music career. In other ways, he was creative and expanding, emotional, and compassionate. I forgave him and, though I didn't cry for six years, I did learn to trust him again.

Dad was an exciting man with a lot of charisma. The way he talked made me feel that I was the only person who mattered in the world. He asked good questions and seemed truly interested in my response. We adored each other and developed a very close and loving relationship. He had pet names for me like 'baby-doll' and 'sweetie-pie'. When I was eight, we sang together at various Legions in the Vancouver area with Taller O'Shea and the Shenanigans. Hearing our voices blend made my heart swell and my skin tingle.

Dad was a giant in my eyes, but in reality, he was around 5'6" with brown hair and blue eyes. He wasn't slight rather he had a stocky build with lots of lean muscle. His eyes twinkled when he was happy and there were laugh lines around them. He often wore blue.

Sometimes, the band played locally at different Supper Clubs. The ones I recall are The Kubla Khan and The Cave. They played dances, weddings, and the Legions, as well.

Dad played the bass, accordion, and was a talented, classical guitarist. His rendition of Ernesto Lecuona's "Malagueña" was impressive.

Dad bought me my first Kodak Brownie Holiday camera and taught me how to use it. He read poems to me that he had written. Some of them were quite profound to a little girl. He introduced me to country music and we both loved it. I had a good ear so Dad taught me how to sing harmony. He was often on the road with the band. I received some letters from him while he was gone, but I missed my father terribly. There was nothing I could do about his lifestyle. I loved my father unreservedly.

When he came off tour, we went fishing and swimming in the Fraser River. We sang at the Legion and walked in the forest. I enjoyed the smell of the wet mouldering earth and hearing the crunch of leaves and twigs as we tramped along. It was during these walks that I grew to love nature especially penny plant, pussy willows, and bull rushes, which grew in the roadside ditches. These plants were in abundance. We picked them to make an arrangement for our dining room sideboard.

Dad worked in the lumber mill when he was home. One time, he got a terrible cedar rash on the inside of his forearms. It nearly drove him around the bend. He sat at the dining room table, forearms up so that mom could put some ointment on his red and inflamed skin.

He was often sore when he came home from the mill, and Mom would rub his back and shoulders with some stinky old white liniment. Blah. I can still smell that darn stuff. It burned my nostrils and put tears in my eyes. It smelled like camphor, turpentine and ammonia. Yuck.

Dad was that elusive guy who came home every few months and brought the world to me. His stories about the places he had been and the things he had seen were riveting. In my eyes, my mom and dad were deeply in love. I thought I would like a marriage like theirs when I got older.

My relationship with my mom was quite different. She was the one who had to be responsible and keep the family together. She was our heart and soul. Mom showed me how to raise children and I had lots of practise. As the eldest of six, I was her partner more than her child. She needed my help, and I gladly shouldered the load.

Mom was a quiet woman determined to do the right thing. She loved her children with all of her heart and wanted each and every one of us. She had a rare sense of humour: sometimes a sailor, and sometimes more subtle. She was tiny with auburn hair and green eyes. My colouring and build is similar to my mom's.

She taught me how to safely light a fire in the wood stove, chop kindling, pump water, separate clothes, load the wringer washer, and hang the clothes out on the line. If it was raining, we lowered the drying rack from the ceiling over the tub and the clothes took shifts drying there. With six children, you can imagine the heaps of laundry that needed to be done. During the winter, I took the frozen clothes off the line and stood them up against the wall of the pantry to defrost. It was funny to look at, and I wish I'd taken some photos of them. These were the types of pictures I liked the most, ones that showed how our lives were lived in that moment.

The smell of our house as I entered the front door was a homey mixture of cedar smoke, clean laundry, and a casserole cooking. This combination of odours can instantly take me back in time to when life was simpler and slower than it is now.

Ironing for a family the size of ours was quite an undertaking. There were enormous piles of it. We had an empty ketchup bottle with holes in the lid to do the 'sprinkling'. I stretched out the largest piece on the ironing board and sprinkled a little warm water on it. Then I added the next biggest piece and sprinkled it. When seven or eight pieces were dampened, I rolled them into a bundle and put it in the basket. Then I started on the next one. Then to iron it all. None of the clothes we wore were 'no-iron' and the iron didn't have a clothes sprayer on in. Dad's stage uniform often included a shirt with ruffles on the front and French cuffs. These were a real challenge to get perfectly pressed. But perfection is what was expected so that is what I delivered.

We baked bread and buns twice a week. The small kitchen was littered with silver pans, which had seen better days. The wood stove was stoked up to 350 degrees Fahrenheit. Flour, lard, and yeast proofs were on every surface. Proofing the yeast (a bowl of yeast, sugar, and warm water) to make sure the bread rises high is a crucial step in the bread-making process. If the water is too hot, it kills the yeast. Too much sugar can inhibit the growth. I learned the alchemy that is bread-making. After the first rise, Mom and I were elbow deep in dough and so warm our cheeks were flushed a fiery red. Brightly coloured cotton cloths covered the heavily-laden pans, which were awaiting their turn in the process.

Several hours later, the table and counters were blessedly burdened with golden brown, butter-topped buns and bread. The aroma filled the house and wafted out into the surrounding neighbourhood. Like the pied piper, it attracted kids from up and down the block. Today, the smell of fresh-baked bakery items still invokes in me feelings of camaraderie with my mother.

Mom taught me how to make a moist chocolate mayonnaise cake, macaroni and cheese, and meatloaf. We didn't have a lot of money but mom knew how to make enough of what we had.

At Christmas, we all got a new dolly. For the smaller dolls, mom made a little rocking cradle out of a Quaker Rolled Oats can. They were round and when laid on their side with half of the topside carefully cut out, they were easily fitted with fabric and a tiny crocheted blanket. The cut-out topside made the rockers. Mom also made the garments for the larger dolls. Intricate crocheted sweaters and slacks were fitted and adorned with matching ribbon. In 1991, my husband, Norman, bought me a "Happy to be Me" doll. Mom made several outfits for it, just like always. It is a gift I still treasure.

Boxes of second-hand clothes arrived on a regular basis. We knew the Johnson family. Ryan, the Dad, was in an iron lung from polio so we never met him. This left 'Auntie' Mary on her own to raise Deirdra, Matilda, and Carly, (all of whom had some problems from polio and asthma) and little Marilyn. We were close to this family and often went to the beach or the movies with them. The kids were all just that much older than us, and we got their hand-me-downs. I loved it when these big boxes of freshly washed clothes and polished shoes arrived. There was always something that was just perfect for me. My sister, Sasha, on the other hand, didn't want to have any of it but, since actual money was so scarce, she had to. I've often wondered if this was hard on her.

I never liked saddle oxfords as much as Victoria, but that is what we had to wear. Each August, when the new school year was almost upon us, Mom took us to downtown New Westminster where Copp's

Shoe store was on the corner of McKenzie and Columbia Streets. The building must have been a hundred years old with high ceilings and shoes in boxes right to the top. Everyone held their breath as the person who waited on us climbed up a sliding ladder and carefully retrieved the desired sizes. A collective outbreath was heard as he put his feet on the floor.

Mom was typically a gentle spirit who also knew how to get our attention if we were doing wrong. One time, when I was really little, she broke her favourite tortoiseshell brush trying to smack me through the bars of my highchair. She didn't hit much but when she did, it really hurt my feelings more than my bottom. Mom's favourite discipline was the dreaded groundings. When I was thirteen, I was grounded for a month for the offense of smoking. This was the most horrible thing she could have done to me, and it still would be. I DO NOT LIKE MY FREEDOM CURTAILED IN ANY WAY.

One of mom's favourite sayings was "Rise and shine for the mornin's fine, and the sun is scorching your eyes out." What a fun way to start my day, laughing. Another thing she liked to say was, "Hold 'er, Nute, she's headin' for the rhubarb!" I never did find out what that meant. But it never failed to make me giggle. She really relished saying, "Whoopi ding. Well, if he wants to whoop his ding, I'll whop it for him!" That one always tickled my funny bone, too.

My love for my mom was quiet and deep. We were a team raising the children and keeping the house tidy. I loved being with her. I'd rather be with her than outside playing. We enjoyed baking, canning, shopping, playing *Canasta*, talking, or going for long drives and outings with the little kids.

My mom was a smoker. No matter where we lived, there was always a cigarette rolling station set up in the corner, which housed rolling papers, a can of fragrant tobacco, a five cigarette rolling machine, and a razor blade to cut the smokes down to size. All of us older kids learned how to do this. The cigarette packet was filled up again and any extras were placed on top of the tobacco, then the plastic was carefully put back and the lid put on the can.

On my first birthday, Mom was in the hospital having had my sister, Victoria, the day before.

On my second birthday, Mom was on the road with my dad. Victoria and I were staying with Winnie Cooper who was a member of the Salvation Army. Her house was on the corner of Sixth Street and Tenth Avenue in New Westminster. The room in which we slept had a piano. I have a hazy memory of someone playing, singing, and smiling at me through the bars of my crib. Though the remembrance is not clear the feeling is, it was joy.

In 1954, my sister, Sasha was born in Edmonton, Alberta. A few months after Sasha was born, we were back in British Columbia and were once more living with Grandma and Grandpa MacKay on Garrett Street. It was there that I endured the measles on my third birthday.

My dad was an entertainer at CKNW in 1955; I remember feeling so proud when I heard him sing on the radio with the Rhythm Pals. Bob Reagan, Elmer Tippy, Evan Kemp, Pappy, and so many others were all a part of our lives during that time. Dad's nickname was Little Bambi. That was the year my sister Catharine was born.

I have a shaky memory of us living in Queensborough in 1956 and can recall one incident when a taxi came to pick us up right in the middle of my *Zorro* program. I was not impressed and made a fuss. The wooden spoon being threatened was enough to get me out the door.

It was at this tiny house that we enjoyed our first television experience. We had what Dad called rabbit ears and an aerial. They were constantly being adjusted. But once that was done, we settled down and watched programs like *I Love Lucy, Loony Toons*, and *The Ed Sullivan Show*. TV was a marvel, and I was hooked at an early age. The land of fantasy and reality TV was right in our own living room. I was five then and by the age of ten, I was hooked on *Sea Hunt* with Lloyd Bridges, *My Three Sons*, and *Bonanza*.

There was a compost heap in our back yard. My Grandpa Harris told me that this pile would get so hot it could burn all the way through the earth to China. He warned me to stay away from it or it would swallow me up and spit me out on the other side of the world. I'd be all alone. I had nightmares about falling in it and being buried alive. Believe me, I did not go near that pile.

We lived on the other side of the tracks and sometimes I thought the train was going to come right through our front door. The kettle used to dance across the stovetop and crash to the floor, spraying hot water everywhere. The plates and bowls rattled in the cupboard. Mom slid knives between the cupboard door handles to keep them closed. Tea towels were used to tie the lower cupboards together. She also jammed table knives in the front door frame to keep the door shut. She became very inventive in order to keep house and home together. This memory brings to mind that old song about a freight train going so fast.

Mom had said I would be going to Queen Elizabeth School for grade one the next year and I was so proud thinking I would be going to the Queen's school. The Queen had visited New Westminster the year I was born and this was a big deal to me. I was heartbroken when we had to move again. I started grade one at Bridgeview

Elementary in Surrey. Through my research I have learned that I attended three schools and lived at four different addresses during that ten-month period.

My brother Joel was born in 1957, while we were living in Surrey. Mom now had five kids under the age of six. She was not yet twenty-four and a half.

When Joel was three days old, he had a brain hemorrhage, which caused some damage. It was suggested to mom that she put him into Woodlands School but she refused saying his place was with the family. He had to take phenobarbital and Dilantin to control the epilepsy. It was a difficult time for my parents, and for us all.

Today, I am so grateful that Mom made this choice. He graduated from high school, bought his own car and has been working for the same company for over twenty years. He is the only person in our family that can make that claim. We are all very proud of Joel and the fine person he has become.

Even though I didn't start school where I wanted to, it was good to be there. This was something for me that I didn't have to share. There were lots of books. I loved to read even at that age. I loved stories and made up my own. I had no comprehension, at this tender age, how important that first introduction to the world of words would be for me. I was being drawn into a powerful place, the place of imagination.

WHERE AM I NOW?

I enjoyed my seventh birthday in a grey-shingled house at the foot of Keary Street in Sapperton. The Lucky Lager Brewery sign is behind me in the photo I have of my birthday party. I started grade two at Richard McBride Elementary School. I remember walking up Keary, across East Columbia for a block, and then up Hospital Street. The school loomed like a castle, foreboding and grey.

We must have been in Sapperton for a few months because I do recall carrying a bowl of orange Jell-O up to the school for a Halloween party. It never made it. I stumbled on a tree root and the Jell-O went flying before it splattered to the ground. I was too far up to go back down and get something else and still get to school on time. So, I stoically climbed the hill empty-handed, save the bowl.

My dad was born in 1929 and lived in Sapperton for the first twenty-three years of his life. That year, Richard McBride Elementary School was rebuilt because the old-school was levelled by a fire. From 1935 until 1941 my father attended school Richard McBride. I didn't know it then but I'm glad to know now that Dad attended the same school as Victoria and I.

I had developed two bad habits at this point in my life. I grabbed the door by the edge instead of by the knob, and I put on my coat in an unusual way.

One day, I didn't remove my fingers fast enough and slammed the door on my own digits. My mom got out the big silver dish in which I soaked my 'wee handies', as Grandma MacKay used to say. I didn't cry. I just fumed inside for being so clumsy.

And, even after being repeatedly warned by my dad against the method, I used to flip my jacket over my head, invariably setting the light bulb to swinging. This really ticked him off. He liked to be obeyed and would sometimes get out the strap if we didn't cooperate in his goal to have a nice quiet house.

But with Dad around, it was never quiet. We often had musicians over for a jam session. I loved to sing, too, and eventually had a career as a Country Rock singer.

The next clear memory I have is being in a one-room school called East Richmond Elementary. My public-school record states that we started there on November 10, 1958. I was in grade two and Victoria was in grade one. One woman taught all seven elementary grades in the same room. Grades eight to ten were being taught in the other room by the principal. There was a ramp between the two buildings.

My sister Victoria, a mischievous redhead, was born left-handed. The teacher was always disciplining Victoria to get her to use her right hand. I suppose Miss Bell had had enough one day. The 'strap' was threatened if Victoria didn't start to use her right hand immediately. I couldn't stand for this. I felt responsible to protect all of my siblings from harm. I pushed Victoria out of the way and took the strap myself.

It was a painful ordeal because now the teacher was really angry at my insolence. She gave me ten hard belts across each hand and actually drew blood. I couldn't write for the rest of the week. Unfortunately for me, corporal punishment was acceptable in those days.

Needless to say, this was enough to traumatize my poor sister into becoming right-handed for the rest of her life. It had a profound effect on her self-esteem.

We were living on the upper floor of a brown wooden building. There were two bedrooms and the four of us girls slept in one while Mom, Dad and our brother, Joel, slept in the other. There was one bathroom and another room, which served as the kitchen and living room. The house sat half over the Fraser River and half on the clay shore. Stilts kept us out of the water. There was a tree filled island across the water, within swimming distance. Log booms filled the area in between. On the other side of the street was a big ditch with some lovely homes behind it, set far back off the road. These boasted lovely flower gardens all season long.

Sometimes the river flooded so Mom or Dad would put a plank out to the road for us to walk on to get to school. I found this very frightening as I had a terrible fear of water.

At night, as I drifted off to sleep, I could hear the water lapping against the pilings supporting our home. I smelled the pungent clay beach into which the poles plunged. This invoked in me a frightening nightmare.

It was always the same. I started out as a happy child wading into the kid's pool. Then the pool turned up-side-down on top of me, and I found myself in a ditch. The water, dirt, and sticks went up my nose and in my mouth. I was freezing cold and I couldn't breathe. I started counting my numbers in an effort to 'remove' myself from the scene but I couldn't concentrate. I felt my chest being crushed. I'd wake up shaking and sweating because I was so afraid. If I cried out, my mom would come in and sit with me but most of the time,

I didn't tell her. I didn't want to burden her or attract attention to myself. She was tired a lot.

Twenty years later, my good friend, Louise Silver, told me a chilling story from her past. We were just getting to know each other in 1974. She told me that a year before my birth, her daughter Tanya had drowned in a ditch outside of her home. There were twigs and clay mud in her nose and mouth as she gulped for air. When Tanya passed over, she was the same age as I was when I started having the nightmare.

The little hairs on my arms and neck stood up as Louise related this event to me only minutes after I had told her my story. 'Weeze' and I were close, but at that point, we started to think of each other truly as spiritual mother and daughter. I'll share more about this relationship in a later chapter.

Mom visited with one of our neighbours up the street and we kids were always in tow. Victoria repeatedly annoyed Lady, the Irish setter, and one day Lady took a chomp out of Victoria's rear end. We thought the wailing would never stop. No one felt sorry for Victoria as she had been warned. Off to the hospital we went on the bus with her butt bleeding everywhere. Sasha thought it was hilarious that a redheaded dog had bit a redheaded kid and kept the story going for years.

When Sasha was born, she had a terrible time nursing. Mom took her to the doctor, and she was diagnosed with Ankyloglossia. She had to have a Lingual Frenectomy to release her tongue as she was, what was known in the day as, tongue-tied. To explain, she had a fold of tissue under her tongue (called a 'frenulum'), which was taut and held her tongue in place. When it was snipped, she was able to properly suckle and later use her tongue correctly to form words. I think everyone in the family knows just how much my dear sister likes to use this organ. She is very chatty.

Her laughing and taunting of Victoria stopped one day when she walked barefoot through the woodpile even after she had been repeatedly told not to. Sasha got a nasty sliver in the bottom of her foot. The howling was fierce. She was laid out on the kitchen table and Dad held her down while Grandpa dug it out. She then received a spanking to punctuate her ordeal. To this day, she still walks around in bare feet. Oh well. (*sigh*)

In 1959, when I was eight, we moved again. Grandpa Harris (mom's dad) had retired with a good pension, which left them rather well off compared to our family. They'd been travelling in Great Britain and needed somewhere to live. They rented a large Craftsman house on London Street in New Westminster and we all moved in together. Our quality of life changed dramatically. We attended Lord Tweedsmuir School.

Thunder rolled through the house in the early morning as my grandfather sat and played his heart out at the piano. I pulled on a robe and flew down the stairs to sit beside him. I watched like an eagle so I could remember where his hands were and what they sounded like on the keys. Listening to my grandpa play the piano brought back memories of joy and safety from my earlier years. I learned how to play Fur Elise and other classical compositions while sitting beside my grandpa on the piano bench.

I enjoyed the special attention I received. I revelled in feeling his right arm over my shoulders, squeezing me when I did a good job. I can still see his left hand showing me the notes on the keyboard. As the eldest of five, I was starving for affection. I loved this man with all of my heart.

He told stories about seeing elephants and tigers at the zoo in London. They showed us pictures of these wild animals, and of the changing of the guard, and Queen Elizabeth of England and Prince Philip, Duke of Edinburgh. This was exciting and exotic stuff for an eight-year-old.

The best part of my grandparents living with us was that our allowance, which had been ten cents a week, was now increased to a quarter. In those days, that would cover a movie and snack, plus bus fair to get there and home.

He and my grandmother were quite elegant and poised. We weren't used to all the glamour or the money that abounded and we enjoyed it. My Grandma Harris was a true lady. She always dressed and acted the part of royalty. She wrote, as well, and reading was her escape from the realities of her life with her husband. My love of words comes to me from several past generations of writers on both sides of my family.

There was an ugly side to all of this, which left me conflicted and in profound confusion. Unbeknownst to me, Grandpa Harris was a pedophile. He had had his way with my mother and now, for over eighteen months, he sexually abused me, too. One of my other sisters suffered the same fate and still has nightmares about it. It's strange that the man I loved, trusted, and worshipped, I also hated, loathed, and wished were dead. When he died of a heart attack in his bed in our home, I wondered if it was my fault. I remember cuddling in my dad's arms, trying to understand it all in my nine-year-old heart while I watched the ambulance attendants carry him down the stairs and out the door.

I sat on my dad's lap and wailed. The floodgates opened. It had been six years since I had cried. Dad held me as I wept out of control. All the pain and confusion about moving around so much, not being able to make any friends, what Grandpa did to me, Dad always being away, being rejected at school because I was overweight, and constantly vying for my parents' attention overwhelmed me completely. I became depressed. All I wanted to do was sleep. I started to miss school so I could stay home and be with my mom because it was the only time I had her to myself. Most of the time, I felt like my life wasn't worth living.

There have been times when I've wondered about my dad's leaving and never coming back. Had he smothered Grandpa in his sleep after finding out what he'd done to his little girls? Was there an investigation into this death? My grandpa was only fifty-seven and died at home in his sleep. Did it get too hot to stay in BC and did Dad have to get lost? Or, am I just a curious person with a vivid imagination?

When I was thirty-eight, I recall asking my mom why she'd let them come live with us since she knew what he was like. Her answer was short and to the point, "Because we needed the money, darling."

It turns out that my mom's little sister had been sent out of the family home to live on the other side of the country so she wouldn't be a target. How did that make my mom feel, to know that she was sacrificed so my aunt wouldn't be touched? How did my mom feel knowing she'd sacrificed at least two of her little girls for the sake of money? These questions haunt me, at times, to this day.

I think of this now and remember that Mom's sister died of heart failure and Mom died of cancer. It was too much for these two little girls to deal with and eventually, it caught up to both of them. For me, it shows as systemic disease in various forms – arthritis, diabetes, fibromyalgia, and lupus, to name a few. It seems I'm still trying to get off this planet, though in a less direct and much more painful way.

I recall a visit with Great-Aunt Em (Grandma Harris' sister) who said to me, "We knew what was going on in that house but couldn't do anything about it." Adults knew. My mom, maybe my dad, Grandma Harris, her sister Em, and my great-uncle Eric, knew. How many adults knew and did nothing about it? I just don't know what to think about this. It hurts my heart.

I've often wondered if Grandpa Harris went after boys, too. Did he go after my uncle (my mom's baby brother)? I wonder, because, when I was twelve, and we were living in Queensborough, my favourite uncle, whom I loved very much, took me out to the PNE for the day. We had an exciting time. We got off the bus on Ewen Ave. and began walking down Wood St. My uncle spun me around, hugging me up in the air, feet off the ground, and French kissed me deeply; it all happened so fast. Then he put me down, held my hand, and walked me home as if nothing happened.

He seemed normal with Mom and my siblings. I was stunned into silence, and my world came crashing down. It was happening again. Who could I trust? I never talked to him again and always avoided him when he was around. I begged off many family get-togethers so I wouldn't have to be around him. I was heartily criticized for this behaviour.

My uncle's eldest son became an alcoholic, too. Did my uncle go after this son? Is that why my cousin committed suicide, or as the coroners' report stated, 'preventable events and circumstances that caused his untimely death'? Is this how the pedophile tracks through families? These questions will never have answers as all the players are dead and gone now. I have to clear my head and move on.

I was usually the new kid in class. In fourth grade at Lord Tweedsmuir, my teacher's name was Miss Grimmer. She brought me into the class to introduce me and then she asked Donna Henshaw to be my buddy. We became good friends for all of grade four.

If she was team captain, there was no problem with me getting a spot on the team. If we were doing it the 'Red Rover' way, I was seldom chosen. Being fat meant I was not even worth knowing, according to most of the kids, and I was teased about it constantly.

I fell in love for the first time when I was nine. His name was Danny and he was just too dreamy to talk about. (*sigh*) I passed him notes in class and drew pictures of him. He became ill one day and had to be taken to the hospital. I drew a little cut-out of him as a get-well gift. I kept it in my desk, awaiting his return to class.

A few days later, Miss Grimmer entered the classroom. She had obviously been crying. She told us that Danny's appendix had exploded and he had died. I had a horrible visual of Danny being splattered all over the walls of his hospital room. Frightened out of my wits, I bolted from the class and ran all the way home clutching my little cut-out of Danny.

Dad was home and once again, I flew into his arms howling and choking. I showed him the cut out, and he chuckled and told me it was cute. I told him he didn't understand, Danny had died and this was all I had left of him. I was heartbroken.

My mom had made a chocolate cake that morning. The smell of it started to make me feel better as soon as I'd run into the house. It tasted dark and moist and sweet. As I ate it, I felt soothed and fell into an almost in a trance-like state. My mom said I'd been a good girl and always so helpful so she offered me another piece, which I consumed with much enthusiasm. I'd found something to comfort me as nothing else could… food.

In our house, as in many others at that time, food was used as a reward, a comforter, and a punishment. We were sometimes sent to bed without our supper if we misbehaved. Conversely, we were promised treats if we performed up to the standards of the task that was required doing.

We ate much better and food was more plentiful when Grandma and Grandpa had come to stay. Food became all mixed up with love, and reward, and raw emotions. Food became my drug of choice, my panacea.

During this dark time in my life, I picked up a little guy on my shoulder. This tiny voice would always remind me that nothing was permanent and that I was not safe. My body went on high alert. I could die at any second. I could be sexually assaulted and betrayed by someone I loved and trusted. Overnight, I could be uprooted from my school and any friendships made. I alternately held on too tightly or let go too soon of the people, places and things that mattered to me most. I started to withdraw emotionally from the world.

Dad had given me a camera for my birthday and that was where I hid most often, narrowly seeing the world through the flat focus of a camera lens. That was only one of the places I learned to hide. In short order, I found that books took me off to far-away places with marvellous people. Writing down my feelings in the form of poetry would while away the hours. Losing myself behind a microphone up on a stage came with the added benefit of applause. I ate my way through grief and confusion and several broken hearts. Finding all kinds of ways to distance myself from my loved ones, I built a tight cocoon around myself and didn't know it. Food and anything else that would dull my emotions became my best friends.

It was a horrible ordeal for me to go back to school the day after Danny died. But Donna was there to comfort and soothe me. I've remembered and cherished her friendship all of these years, although I have no idea where she is or even if she is still alive.

In this big house on London Street, we had room to spare. Instead of being three to a bed or four to a room, we were just two to a room in our own bed and we had our own dresser and closet space.

I used to stay awake singing and daydreaming after we were put to bed. I had a fantasy that there was a man in the closet with a microphone and a recorder who realized what a talented singer I was. He would jump out and tell me so. Then he would promise to take me away and make me a star. This always made me smile and drift off to sleep knowing that, one day, I would be able to prove myself and become somebody people would admire and love and want to be with.

Sometimes my sister, Victoria, and I would get to talking and Dad would bound up the stairs two at a time and holler, 'One more peep out of any of you and I'll get the wooden spoon!' We, of course, would all go 'peep, peep, peep' and we could hear him chuckling all the way down the stairs.

Winnie Cooper was still taking us to Sunday school each week no matter where we lived. Up to this point in my life, we had moved over a dozen times. She was a desperately needed constant in our fragmented lives. The spiritual underpinnings from this experience are, I believe, what have kept me going in life. For eight years, from the time I was two until I was ten, she took us all to the Salvation Army.

We learned to pray, love God and Jesus, and believe in Angels that were around us. She was a shining example of the goodness in the world. I was young and self-absorbed, so I don't remember too much about her. Thankfully, what I do remember is a feeling of joy, passion, and purpose from her. She was an epitome of a giving person. This lesson would do me well in my life. I wanted to be like her.

My parents made sure that we were all baptized and attended church regularly. They, however, did not come with us. My dad wanted to join the local Baptist church as he loved gospel music but they wouldn't have him due to his profession as an entertainer. He stayed away from churches after that.

Our family of four girls and one little boy moved to Laidlaw Street in Ladner where I completed grade five and started grade six at Ladner Elementary. In all, I changed schools nine times during my first seven years of education, twice going back to a school I had previously attended. It was difficult to make and maintain friendships, so I didn't.

My sister Claire was born on January 31, 1962 while we were living in Ladner. This is the only birth of a sibling that I remember clearly.

Mom had gone to take a nap. She had to lie down often as her water had broken a month before. Mom and Dad had taken to calling the unborn child Murgatroyd. Mom let out a holler and called "Jeremy!" Dad raced up the stairs. The time had come. Mom was going to have a baby. All of us were so excited.

Dad carried her down the stairs and out to our black Morris Minor. Off they went to Vancouver General Hospital to have our sweet baby Claire. She was such a smiley little person. We all loved to take care of her, except for the yucky diapers. She was our real live dolly, and we were thrilled to have her.

Over the summer, we often packed up a picnic lunch and drove to Point Roberts, White Rock, or Crescent Beach for the day. It was quite a procedure to prepare for this colossal event. The day before, we baked a chocolate layer cake, fried chicken, and boiled the potatoes and eggs.

The following morning, Mom frosted the cake. My sisters and I chopped the eggs and potatoes, grated the carrots, and snipped the green onions. We filled the big Dutch oven about three quarters of the way up and mixed in the Miracle Whip, salt, pepper, and paprika. After Mom finished icing the cake, she made a few dozen deviled eggs. We placed the food into the hamper then added some tea towels, ice, pickles, Kool-Aid, and freshly baked bread. We also had a Tupperware container of wet face cloths for washing up. The cake went into a big Tupperware cake-saver of which Mom, and only Mom, was in charge. There was a lot of preparation to feed seven people on a picnic.

I sat in the passenger seat with baby Claire in my arms. Victoria, Sasha, Catharine, and Joel filled the back seat of our little car and away we'd go. Since there were no seat belt regulations, we could all squish in with very little problem.

We sang "Teddy Bear's Picnic", "My Grandfather's Clock", "Hey Look Me Over", "Does Your Chewing Gum lose its Flavour", and many other tunes. We drove along with the windows open and the air whipping our hair into strange dos. Sometimes, one of us would have a pinwheel but it would invariably fly out the window.

We played car games like 'spot the red car', 'I spy', and 'how many so-and-so's (whether that be hawks, fence posts, or whatever) can you count?'

One time, the radiator blew on the way to White Rock. Mom passed around chewing gum and ordered us to chew it into large gooey wads. Meanwhile, she got out the aluminum foil she'd packed to rewrap the food. She carefully placed the foil over a small hole, stuck it there with the gum and filled up the radiator with the Kool-Aid we had in a pitcher in the trunk. We saw nothing wrong with this procedure.

It worked well enough to get us back home. We had our picnic on the living room floor.

On October 12, 1962, Typhoon Freda hit the west coast of British Columbia with a furious blow. This date is forever etched in the minds of our family because my mom's sister Selena got married to Chas Roland that day.

Before she could carry on to the wedding, Mom and my sister, Sasha, went to pick up baby Claire, who was visiting with a family friend, and bring her home to be with me. On the way to get Claire, the car door flew open and the vehicle started to lift into the air. It settled back on the road and they carried on.

Mom was the Matron of Honour so had to leave me with my five siblings and my cousin, Gertie (Selena's daughter). How none of us perished, I'll never know. Off she went in the Morris with the wind whipping around her and pulling on the doors of her car. Remember there were no seat belts in those days.

I was in stark terror with the sheer responsibility of the task; the dog was peeing everywhere, barking, and running up and down the stairs. The kids were shrieking in fear. The storm was howling. The noise was incredible. The windows were swaying inward and creaking, threatening to burst, so I told the kids to go and get the mattresses off the beds. They dragged them down the stairs. We stood them up against the front room windows and held them there with the dining room table and sideboard. The leftover ones were put on the floor in the middle of the room and there we all huddled together.

I was sick with worry about my mother being out in this storm. She had to drive from Ladner to New Westminster and back again. I didn't want to look out the window in case what I saw was too horrible to absorb. It's the sound of it that I remember. We lived in Ladner in a century-old house that had seen better days fifty years earlier. I wondered if it would continue to hold us. I concentrated my efforts on protecting the kids and our home. I was eleven.

When mom came home several hours later, we were all crowded together around the kitchen table by the wood stove. The power had gone off. The tears were streaming down our faces. The porridge was steaming up in front of us. Mom always remarked that she wished she'd had a camera to take a photo of this woeful scene, her little waifs. I've never eaten porridge again. It gets stuck in my throat and I gag.

The next day was a wonder, sunny and bright. We all walked up and down Trunk Road and couldn't believe our eyes. Houses were flattened. Trees were up-rooted. A coke bottle was stuck in a telephone pole. People were wandering around dazed. A blade of grass stuck out an oak tree. There were wires dangling everywhere. It was dangerous but we didn't know it. We were simply fascinated with the juxtaposition of these everyday items.

When our electricity came back on, we watched the news for pictures of the things we'd witnessed. By all accounts, it was touted as the storm of the century, killing forty-five people and flattening billions of board feet of timber from Northern California to British Columbia, costing millions.

Called the 'Columbus Day Storm' in the United States, it was considered to be the most damaging mid-latitude cyclone that has hit the coast in the last one hundred years. And, our little troupe survived it!

Aunt Selena and Uncle Chas' wedding day went off without a hitch and Mom returned safely home.

Ten days later, the same TV newscaster had an even deadlier report. The showdown between Kennedy and Khrushchev regarding the missiles in Cuba was scaring the pants off of everyone. A compromise was reached and nuclear war was barely avoided.

This sort of news gets terribly distorted in the mind of a child. It certainly was in mine. I got it in my brain that missiles were going to fly through the sky and land on our heads, blowing us all up. I felt frightened when I heard airplanes.

At school, we had drills where we had to quickly get under our desks. There was another drill where we had to leave the school and briskly walk to an underground building close by. Nothing was really explained to us, that I recall. The adults all looked scared yet business-like. It was difficult to know what to feel.

I had to walk through a park to get to my school. One day I heard a plane overhead and thought it was one of those missiles. I hit the grass on my stomach and bellied over to the trees where I hid in fear, shook, and vomited for the balance of the day. When night started to fall, I walked home still dazed from my ordeal. I have no memory of what happened when I reached the safety of my family.

Repressed memories and emotions are a significant theme in my life. I found out later in life that this is how children and young adults sometimes deal with traumatic events.

Even given all of these incidents, Ladner was the place I loved the most. My memories are clear and the good feelings and experiences have travelled with me through the years.

Mom and I often played *Canasta* for a few hours after the little kids had gone to bed. I loved getting the big discard pile and I'd run into the dining room to sort it. I yelled, "Don't come in here, Mom!" and she'd run down the hall through the front room and open the French doors threatening to come in. The cards were too many for me to hold and I often dropped them. Sometimes I laid them out in facedown piles on the table in front of me. We knew how to have a good time in a simple way.

Invariably we would want a snack and she'd send me out to the Blue Bird Café for a candy bar for each of us. Or, we may have made some cinnamon toast and hot chocolate or some hot buttered popcorn done up on the wood stove. This was our special time together. I have nourished these types of memories over all the other crap that filled my life.

It's the silliness, the laughter that I remember the most. One spring day, Mom made the dreaded tomato aspic. We all hated it but mom made it anyway. This time, when she placed the plate on top to flip it over, it slipped and went skidding across the floor. Our little doggie sure enjoyed it. We laughed and laughed.

We started attending the United Church across the road and I enjoyed singing the hymns and hearing the sermon. The grownups were always trying to get me to go downstairs for Sunday school with the little kids. But I was eleven and I thought I was pretty grown up since I had just survived a typhoon with six kids under my wing. I held my ground and was allowed to stay. Sometimes we had bread and grape juice. I loved to pray and find out more about God and Jesus. My favourite hymns were "Fairest Lord Jesus", "Jesus Loves the Little Children", "Holy, Holy, Holy", and "How Great Thou Art".

It was here, at this house, that mom got some battleship grey paint and painted all of the floors. Then she took red, yellow, and green paint and three sponges and worked a creative pattern all over the floors. She was ahead of her time in home decorating, for sure. It really looked cool and we were proud of the job she had done. It also wore down into an interesting lived-in pattern.

We lived next door to the Fenton's. I was sitting on the back steps, shelling peas with Mrs. Fenton, when this funny song came on the radio. It was "Barbara Ann". It took me a while to get used to the words but once I did, I loved that song. I loved almost anything that was unusual or different in some way. Mrs. Fenton and I enjoyed a little dance then went back to our peas.

One day, my friend Margaret W. was over visiting. She was such a sweetie. We really gravitated to each other. We were best friends for over a year. Anyway, on this day, David, a boy from my sixth-grade class, walked by. I knew he liked me but I wasn't too sure about him. Neither was our black lab, Akeila, who growled and barked up a storm. Skirting the dog, he walked into our back yard and sat on the swing. Margaret and I continued to talk and did not pay any attention to him. She left a little while later and David said he would like to push me on the swing, so I accepted. He pushed for a while and then he abruptly stopped the swing and kissed me on the mouth. I was so mortified; I ran inside and hid in my room. I vowed I would never let another boy kiss me like that. That was my first kiss by a boy my own age.

Another first was wrought on me by Albert, Margaret's older brother, who thought it was okay to show his eighteen-year-old penis to an eleven-year-old girl. Again, I was dumbfounded and ran home, hiding in my room for hours. I couldn't talk about such things to anyone. What was with men and their unwarranted flagrant violations of my person? I felt ashamed of myself like I'd done something wrong. Go figure.

This has always been a questions that's haunted me and I would love to have an answer one day – Why do the 'abused' feel ashamed? They've done nothing wrong. The abuser goes about their everyday life like nothing's happened. They don't appear to be ashamed. What's the deal here?

With Dad in the entertainment business, we met and had in our home some of the Country Music stars of the time including Marty Robbins, Carl Smith, and Lucille Starr to name a few. I learned how to sing "The French Song" in honour of 'Aunt' Lucille. I was just a kid then, but I knew enough to determine who 'had it' and who didn't. She did. Oddly, thirty years later, my husband and I bought a home, which was close to Lucille Starr Drive.

Wanting to go into the business myself, I was always an eagle eye observing how to act and learning what to respond to certain questions. I became versed in how to carry and express myself in a warmly professional way on stage. Dad taught me what to do with the jitters and how to get a crowd going. I put it all to good use later in my life. I loved entertaining. I'd still be doing it, if that were in the stars for me. But I've always had an issue with my energy levels.

Life was not all stage people. We had down-to-earth friends, as well. We knew the Woodward family... Sam, Isabella, Roger, and Daryl. A few months before the Typhoon Freda, Daryl had had open-heart surgery. He laid in his bed during the storm and watched their new roof fly over the treetops. This is the family that baby Claire had been with before Mom and Sasha picked her up only hours before. So glad she was at home with me. Our house stayed in one piece.

The first time I saw 'Uncle' Sam, I immediately got a crush on him. Then I met Roger a few minutes later, and my heart was gone. I think a few of my sisters had a similar reaction. He was a real dreamboat.

Isabella was Italian and quite a joker. I always thought she was cool as she had some interesting ways about her. She salt and peppered her hair; a process whereby a rubber cap is donned and some of her black hair was pulled out through the tiny holes and then streaked grey. She also had plastic covering her turquoise furniture in the living room and we weren't allowed to sit in there. She loved to lounge in a bubble bath with a turquoise princess phone perched on the edge. She chatted away the hours.

Roger and Daryl both passed away from AIDS. Roger was one of the first to go during the original crisis in the early eighties. Daryl followed a few years later. Both were artistic, creative, and loving individuals. Auntie Isabella suffered a break down and immersed herself in her new religious lifestyle, leaving Uncle Sam to figure it out for himself. I don't know where she is today. We are still friends with Sam who has married again to a lovely lady named Greta. They are people we really enjoy spending time with.

I have a fond memory of Isabella. I was nine and we were in the laundromat one day. I had run out of underwear and wasn't wearing any. Mom told Isabella. So, when the dryer stopped, she rummaged through it and gave me a nice warm pair to slip on. I protested that I didn't want to do it in public. She took off her coat and made a blind for me to slip behind. It was so lovely to put on a warm pair of panties in the dead of winter... a really luxurious feeling.

In November 1962, Dad called Mom from Minneapolis to tell her to sell all of our belongings and buy train tickets for the whole family. We were going to be with Dad and tour with him in the U.S. After two years of stability in Ladner, we were off again.

After Grandpa Harris passed over and Grandma Harris went into a community home for the elderly, we acquired some of their larger pieces of furniture. My mom had to sell her parents piano, dining room suite, and sideboard. She sold our living room furniture and all of our beds and dressers, kitchen table and chairs. She bought seven tickets for Minneapolis, and off we went to the train station in New Westminster. It was a dark November day as one by one we climbed the snow-covered steps and were once again off into an uncertain future.

There was no money for sleeper lounges, so we slept in the passenger cars and ate sandwiches Mom had brought along. When that was gone, the Porter was kind enough to bring a big bucket of sandwiches from the galley and some milk for the little kids.

We arrived a few days later and when I got off the train, I felt like I was still on it. My legs were wobbly. Dad and his friend Tiger met us at the train station. Who was this 'Tiger' woman? "Why was she looking at my dad that way? Can you imagine how my mom felt? She'd just sold every possession she had. Now she was in a strange city with six kids, and a cheating husband. I really felt for her and, for the first time, I hated my dad. They'd been married twelve years at that point. He'd always cheated on her.

He was working at the Flame Supper Club in downtown Minneapolis and we had to get home and settled so he could go to work.

I had never seen such a large house as the one which we were renting. It was all white with red carpeting and lots of built-ins. There was a long dreamed-about window seat where I could sit and read. Christmas was fast approaching. It already felt really festive due to the house décor. But this feeling was short-lived. Some sort of tension was brewing in our family. I could feel it. I didn't have a name for it and that made me uneasy. I slowly climbed the stairs of this gorgeous house and found my mattress on the floor. Quite overcome with feelings of dread and foreboding, I wept to the sounds of "Listen to the Rhythm of the Falling Rain". I was scared.

We started school at Warrington Elementary and found that we were the only white kids in a sea of black faces, save one—David Kellogg. Our teacher was also Caucasian. I didn't have a problem with this as I had been around people from everywhere in the world. Canada was known for its multiculturalism, even back then. We were brought up to accept other people's looks, languages, diets, and customs.

We were introduced around as the new kids, again. Things seemed to be going fine until after school. I had heard about one girl whose parents were white and black. She really took exception to me. On the way home, she pushed me in the snow and buried my face. This scared me. She told me not to tell and for some reason, I didn't.

The next day, she'd gotten a bunch of other girls and boys together and they all chased us home. Then, one time, we were caught. I don't know what happened to the rest of the kids, but I was punched and kicked. I didn't want to go back to school. If it hadn't been for the fact that I had a huge crush on David, I wouldn't have. I'd have skipped out.

David was shy and soft-spoken. He had dark hair and wore glasses. He wanted to kiss me. Well, I'd already gone through all that in Ladner and I wasn't at all sure I wanted to try it again. He said the goofiest thing and I agreed to it. He said it would be fun if we were to stick our heads under a lampshade (not attached to a lamp) and kiss there. I thought it was weird, but I did it anyway. He wasn't too bad a kisser, for a twelve year old.

We were almost caught by Mom who hollered for me from the top of the basement stairs. I ran up the stairs and into the bathroom to splash some water on my face and compose myself. David must have slipped out the basement door.

Mom and we kids were invited to go to the Flame Supper Club to see Taller and Dad play. He had said that Kitty Wells was going to be singing. I just loved her music, and so did the rest of the girls. Dad wanted Kitty to come out and meet us but she refused saying a bar was no place for children. It was a fabulous show with Carl Smith, Kitty Wells, and Taller O'Shea and the Shenanigans.

On the news, I heard about some boys that had started up a group called the Black Panthers. It was said that they filed their teeth into points and fell from the treetops onto little children. That was the end of me going out after dark. Mom didn't want me to go out then anyway, so it ended up being a good excuse to stay home. This, of course, was simply propaganda as they were actually a political party.

It was cold and snowy in Minneapolis. With the mighty Mississippi River on one side and snow-capped mountains on the other, it was truly a scenic city but it was too hard for me to live there with so much hate and fear.

Dad and Taller got a job in Billings, Montana a few months later, and we were off again. The car ride was horrible with eight of us packed into a station wagon with all of our stuff. I don't remember much at all about Billings. It was hot. We lived at the foot of a yellow bluff. Everything was dusty. I didn't want to go to school at all. I don't recall if I actually did go to school there. I'd had about enough of this moving around and never staying anywhere long enough to make friends or create some ties in the community. I wanted some stability.

Many times during our childhood, my siblings and I woke up in a house different from the one in which we had fallen asleep. We didn't know where we were or where our stuff was or if we would ever again see a friend we might have made at the last place. We didn't know if Dad would be able to find us or if he was sleeping with Mom downstairs. It was an extremely disconcerting way to live.

It wasn't until I was thirty-three that the penny dropped. I said to my Mom, "We moved nine times during the first seven years I was in school. I know a couple of those times we were with Dad in the States. But most of the schools were in the same area. Most of them were in the same school district. It's not as if we went from Manitoba to British Columbia to Nova Scotia like an Army brat would have to do. Why did we move around so much?"

My parents had never discussed their finances with us. I knew my mom was on welfare, at times. We always looked forward to the nineteenth of the month when we could enjoy the simple abundance of bananas, cookies, and chocolate milk. We didn't have a lot of extras. It never occurred to me, however, that they couldn't pay the rent and had to move in the dead of night so no one could find them. Mom always had a good sense of humour about her hardships. She said simply, "Haven't you ever heard of 'midnight moves', daughter?"

In April 1963, we moved back to Queensborough where we had lived some seven years before. I completed grade six and went through all of grade seven at Queen Elizabeth Elementary School.

Shortly after the 'deep French kiss' from my uncle, I developed this weird illness. I don't think one thing has anything to do with the other except maybe I was exhausted and totally stressed out. My whole body became covered in scabby weeping sores, almost as big as a quarter, from my scalp to between my toes. I had a high fever. It was never determined what it was. It lasted for a few months and left me tired and worn out for several months after that. If I had some sort of treatment for it, I don't recall what it was. It was at that point that I started to have trouble with achy joints and what I called 'the exhausteds'. Often I felt like I had the flu even though no one else around me was sick. I'd be so wiped out, I wouldn't be able to get up from the bed or the couch. I'm fairly certain that this is the event that precipitated the lupus, which was diagnosed some years thirty-five later in 1998.

I often babysat the neighbourhood kids and was driven home, late at night, by the Dads of said children. On three separate occasions, three of these so-called Dads thought it totally appropriate to drive me down by the river and slide their hand up my skirt, then grab my head hair to kiss me. I tried to scream but couldn't get out any sound. The ice that ran through my veins was chilling. The thoughts that ran through my head were not ones I wanted to have. I started to believe that I wasn't a good person and had done something horrendous to deserve this shabby treatment. I told my mom but I think she felt as powerless as I did to do something about this. I felt my only choice was to stop babysitting. That put a real damper on my income as well as my independence.

On the November 22, 1963, at 11:16 a.m., Mr. Moore came into our classroom with a grave look on his face. He said that President Kennedy had been shot and killed. School was dismissed. He was clipped in his speech, and one could see he was quite choked up. He told us we were excused from classes, so I went straight home to see what had happened.

My dad was sitting at the kitchen table crying and writing furiously. The news was on the TV. He said that the President had been shot and the nation was in turmoil.

When Mom and the rest of the kids got home, we watched the news in silence. People that one would not ordinarily see cry, were. ie: Walter Cronkite. By the next day, Dad had completed the following poem:

"Last Taps to John Kennedy"

In the year of 1963, on November 22,
our beloved President, J. F. Kennedy made history anew.
For on that day, he left his home and flew in a fast jet plane
to a place called Dallas, Texas, on a Presidential Campaign.
At the airport a crowd of heart-warmed people gave out with
ringing cheers
as the President and his First Lady, from the plane appeared.
Shouts went up "Hey, Jackie!" They were happy, John and his wife.
No one knew at that moment it was his last day of life.
As he rode through Dallas mid a cheering, milling throng
three shots rang out from a coward's gun and a truly great man was gone.
They rushed him to the hospital to try and save his life, and Jackie
was there,
right beside him, as she had been through all their life.
They worked so hard to save him but in vain, for his life did flow
through the wound from a coward's gun, and a Nations head bent low.
The world has joined together now, in this moment of deep despair.
Men from every country came to offer their last prayers.
And through it all brave Jackie carried on with head held high
for she knows, as doth this Nation, John Kennedy will never die.
He did in death what he tried in life, joined together a world torn apart.
Nations, once bitter, stood side by side, with grief in every heart.
And through the generations, the story of John Kennedy will be told.
To show the world that "Great men live on and on till the flame of
freedom in every corner of the world will so brightly burn."
So sleep well, rest in peace, John Kennedy.
You've made your aim in life come true.

We'll soon have peace on earth and good will towards all.
And we owe it all to you.

"Thanks, Dad, wherever you are, for such an inspiring poem. I couldn't
have said it better myself, so I won't even try."

"I Cry"

I cry for the child who was lost in me
who grew up so fast, could never be free
was always in fear, even in her family
from the time she was little, around age of three
who's struggled and tried so valiantly
to keep herself out of insanity

PUNCHED, BORED, OR REAMED

J ust around my thirteenth birthday, we moved again, to 9th Street at 3rd Avenue in New Westminster. I was to start high school that year at New Westminster Senior Secondary School. Two schools, Lester Pearson High and Vincent Massey Junior High, had amalgamated to form NWSS with over thirty-five hundred kids. An enclosed catwalk bridged the buildings, and it was there, in a long row, that our lockers were housed.

Paul, who lived across the street from us, had promised to walk me to school on my first day. When I went to meet him outside, he was a block ahead of me with some of his friends. They were laughing and pointing back at me. I felt small as I walked to school alone.

First days were always traumatic for me. Sometimes I would hyperventilate. Then I felt dizzy and disoriented. My heart hammered against my chest wall and I perspired like crazy. I thought I was having a heart attack. I wanted to bolt but was glued to the spot. This happened to me over and over during my lifetime.

I found the auditorium where the assembly started at 9:00 a.m. This was held to orient the eighth-graders. I felt completely overwhelmed. I didn't know any of the kids and probably just trudged on through the day, as was my way.

Because I loved reading and wrote constantly, I spent most of my afternoons at the New Westminster Public Library. I can remember the smell of it so clearly and never failed to get excited as I walked through the door. I was in a reading circle and sat with rapt attention listening to the reader. She made the book come to life with her tones of various kinds. Books were the love in my life.

It was a dark, cold day in December 1964. I always cut through Moody Park to go home from school. I'd heard them laughing over by the swings. I was in the middle of a stand of trees. I tried to be quiet but could not. The ground was covered with old snow, and I knew my footsteps were making crunching sounds. They noticed me and, as a group, moved towards me. I froze, paralyzed with fear. I could neither run nor call out. These four men sexually assaulted me.

I recognized one of the men as someone I knew from Queensborough. They taunted me, and for the next space of time, each one of them had a turn on me. They did terrible things to me that a little girl should never even know about. The men held me down but didn't hit me. When they flipped me over, they shoved my face in the snow. They were strong. I smelled alcohol on their breath. I don't know if I screamed. There was nobody there to hear me or help me even though I was only yards away from Century House.

Mercifully, details and total recall are still not completely forthcoming. It was such a traumatic ordeal that my conscious mind could not encompass it, and I immediately repressed the event. I still get new bits and pieces in flashbacks from time to time.

I didn't remember it at all until I was twenty-two, some nine years later. It has taken years of therapy to integrate this event into my consciousness and be able to come to a place where I can write these simple paragraphs and not want to throw up, run away, or just go out of my mind.

I can tell you, now, that when I got home everyone was in the kitchen, which was well in the back of the house. I called out that I was going to have a bath. I put my clothes in the garbage right after the bath. I was in a daze and these memories that I have now are like watching a movie that was taped in slow motion in the fog.

I have queried my mom and my siblings about this, and no one recalls anything unusual during that time period. I must have just gone to bed and left before anyone else got up. I often went off on my own in the morning, so I could smoke, think, and write in peace. Then I probably just kept putting one foot in front of the other as has been my way all of my life.

Though the event was not remembered, it changed me immediately and dramatically. Once a cooperative and helpful person to my mom, I became rebellious and withdrawn. The following February, two months later, I was found by two police officers as I was standing on the railing of the Patullo Bridge. I remember looking at the icy, inky water below and just wanting to be swallowed up in it. I wanted peace. I couldn't understand my behaviour or myself. I hated myself.

I thought I was losing my mind for some reason that I couldn't fathom. The police took me into custody and called the Child Welfare people. The long and the short of this story is that in March 1965, my mom was called unfit to raise me and I was put in a foster home at Saint Judith's rectory in Sapperton. I have always felt so badly about this because she was a good mom.

I remember riding in a car with a lady from this office. She was saying bad things about my mom. We were going down East Columbia Street and passed Woodlands. I knew Mom wasn't bad because she didn't give my brother away and she did so many other good things for us and was always there even when Dad wasn't. This woman was taking me away from the only security I had ever known. Due to our circumstances, I was never able to find security in a place. I had found it in a person-my mom. I had never met these people and I didn't know what it would be like living with them. I was completely powerless in this situation. This made me angry.

I was taken to live with The Reverend and Mrs. K. M. Dark. The woman of the house threw me in a bath of Detol then scrubbed me with a floor brush. She ordered me to remove my nail polish, then she cut back my nails and chopped off my hair. I don't know why she did this. I guess she thought I was a sinner. I started to act the part and became completely boy crazy. I was just looking for love in all the wrong places. I missed my family so much that I cried myself sick on many occasions.

It was then that I started drinking. I drank every chance I got. I was a member of AYPA, Anglican Young People's Association. We had some parties where I got completely loaded. I remember throwing up on the side of the road on the way home then staying in bed for a few days saying I had the flu. As intelligent as these people were, I was never found out.

I was given the opportunity of taking piano lessons. Learning how to read music was daunting. I was quite overwhelmed with other things, so I cheated myself out of learning this skill. I used to coo to Mrs. Nelson, "That is so lovely. Won't you please play it again?" When she did, I would watch her like an eagle and see where she started on the keyboard. Then I would learn how to play it by ear. I got to grade eight in Classical piano just this way. I can read the notes separately, but not the page as a whole. It is definitely my loss, and I regret this lack of commitment and foresight on my part.

Except for that, there is not a lot of good that I can say about the following three years and seven months. I spent a lot of time by myself, listening to records and writing in my diary. The library became a second home to me. Since the other kids living in the house went there, too, I had witnesses to where I was after school.

The law forbade me to see my mom. But in 1967, she moved about two blocks away from where I was living. I started to leave a little earlier for school so that I could have breakfast with my family. It was soothing to be with them once more.

What I had thought was a loving union between my parents had been a farce. My dad was unfaithful to my mom right from the start. He and mom would go for a drive quite often. I thought they were out on a date or wanting some privacy. I found out years later that this is where they went to fight about the other women he had been seeing since the beginning of their marriage. I lost faith in my ability to believe what I was seeing with my own eyes, as a result of this discovery. My future relationships suffered because of this.

The January before I was put in foster care, Dad and I went for a walk to the Blue Bird corner store for an ice-cream cone. He talked about someone he met who put the sunsets to shame as she was so gorgeous. At the crosswalk, he asked me if I could keep a secret, even from my mom. I said 'no' and told him it was unfair of him to ask me. He apologized. I never found out what he wanted to say to me. That was the last time I ever saw him.

A few months later, I had a call from my dad. He said he wouldn't be able to see me anymore and that my mom had something to tell me so I'd better phone her right away. What a coward he turned out to be. I did call her, and she told me Dad had found someone new and would now be with her and not with us anymore. Her name was

Cathy. A few years later, Cathy's son died in an alcohol-related car accident, and she never recovered. She took to booze. Obviously, she was of no use to Dad anymore and, as was his way, he left her.

I found out my mom was pregnant. She went full term to the August 16, 1965 and then the baby died at birth. The cord was wound around his neck. He strangled on his way out of the birth canal. His name was Darren John MacKay. There was no burial or memorial. Years later, I asked Mom what had happened to him after he had died. She said she had no money so she had let the hospital take care of him. Mom was always extra full of milk for her babies, and this time was no different. She pumped her breast milk for the babies who were preemies while she was in the hospital. When she went home, she continued to do this for a few weeks and took it back to the hospital every day.

It was my foster mother who told me that my brother had died. She was so cruel. She said that it was a blessing because my mom had too many kids already and look what happened to me – I'd tried to kill myself. I ran upstairs and threw myself on the bed, sobbing. This was a really hard time in my life. There was no one I could talk to. I was fourteen and didn't yet have a best girlfriend to see me through these tough times.

I joined the choir at school, and it was there that I felt the most normal. Singing took me away from myself. Being a part of a group and learning to blend and sing, as one voice, was wonderful for me. I felt like I finally fit in and had value. I also joined the choir at church and loved to sing the hymns and give praise through my voice.

I wrote my dad long letters and sometimes he replied. I had those letters for a long time and read them every so often. Each time we talked, he would call me "Baby Doll". I lapped it up. I was desperate for love and attention. I missed him terribly and blamed myself for what had happened. Would he have left if I had agreed to keep his secret? Was the secret he wanted to tell me that he'd found out what Grandpa had done to us and had come to the rescue of his girls but now had to hide out in the US? This was a chilling thought that haunted me for years.

These times, talking to my dad, gave me hope that I may again see him one day. Though he constantly broke his promises to me of sending letters, gifts and photos, I always had to believe in him. I continued to hold hope in my heart.

I'd received a new Lark camera for my fifteenth birthday and had been taking lots of photographs with it. It would take both colour and black and white film. This was a real thrill for me. The people I was living with went on a lot of outings to the beach, for picnics in the park, or to museums. There were always plenty of opportunities to use my new camera.

I had met a couple of girls at school and we chummed around a lot. Cathy C. was a year ahead of me. She was a big blonde beauty with a wacky sense of humour and a laugh that made me laugh. We had lots of fun together. I started to come out of my fog. Her mom and dad owned and managed an apartment building on Hospital Street just off Columbia Street in Sapperton.

Jeannie B. had moved over from Campbell River and was in my grade. Her brother Gord was good company when he came to visit them. Jeannie was lively and vivacious, just a real joy to be around. She lived with her sister Flora P., her brother-in-law, Andy and their son, David. I have recently renewed my friendship with these two women, Flora and Jeannie.

The three of us, Cathy, Jeannie, and I, loved to party and there was always booze around. I don't recall what their drinking habits were. I didn't care how much they drank or didn't drink. I just made sure I had my stash. I hid some just for me and snuck drinks whenever I could. It didn't take a lot to get me drunk and for that I was truly grateful. My supply lasted a long time.

We were known as the three Musketeers. Jeannie lived on Rousseau Street in Sapperton. On school days, she left her house, walked up to Hospital Street and met Cathy. Then they would walk down East Columbia Street to the rectory and hook up with me. The three of us would walk to 8th Street and 8th Avenue to NWSS, talking and laughing all the way. It didn't matter what the weather was, this was our private time, and we took every advantage to be together.

We were really good friends, and this was the best experience of my teen years. I have looked for Cathy C. over the years but have not been able to connect with her, yet. Jeannie and Flora were at my fiftieth birthday party a few months ago.

That year, 1966, was a banner year in my life. I was singing again, I'd made friends with some great gals, and I did my work experience at a photo lab in downtown New Westminster. It was my responsibility to trim the school photos. I learned so much and was absolutely thrilled to be working there.

There were some humiliating times, which all teens go through. Here is a piece I wrote about my most embarrassing moment...

"Tucked In For The Night"

"I can hardly believe that over thirty years have gone by. I was absolutely mortified then, but I can laugh now.

I'd met Chris at the church group I belonged to. He was everything I ever wanted in a man—tall, dark hair, and he made me laugh. He loved music, as I did. Our favourite song was "Snoopy and the Red Baron". We often played it on the jukebox as we shared a banana split at the Woolworth's counter in New Westminster.

Chris had asked me to go to the Christmas pageant and dance. It was fast approaching, and I didn't have a proper dress for the occasion. I was sixteen and experiencing much anticipation about my first real date. My foster mom and I chose mint green taffeta for the A-line dress with a green chiffon overlay. It had a sash at the neck, and I felt like a queen wearing it. The dress complimented by auburn hair and green eyes. Chris said "What a knock-out!" when he picked me up. So I knew he approved.

We saw our friends as we arrived at the dance. They'd saved us a seat at their table. Chris brought me a coke and a plate of chips for the gang. We danced, talked, laughed, and sang. I was in heaven.

About half way through the evening, a few of us had to use the ladies' room. There was a line-up, but this was just an excuse for more visiting. We were finally able to accomplish our task. I was the last one out. There were four stairs leading down to the dance floor. The boy's bathroom was directly across from ours.

I heard some guys laughing as I descended the stairs. They spoke my name so I turned to them. My backside was now facing the dance floor, and the whole room was howling. Unfortunately, my pretty green dress was tucked into my girdle. My girlfriends came running up to me and started pulling it out. I couldn't understand what was going on. When I realized what had happened, I made a hasty retreat to Chris's car and waited for him there. He came right out, and we had a long talk. We drove around until we found an A&W that was open. We had a burger and a root beer shake. I began to feel calmer.

Chris was a good guy. He was gallant and saw me through a rather rough time in my life. We both found someone else but stayed friends for a while. I'm really glad he was there for my most embarrassing moment."

The following year, Jeannie had to go back to Campbell River and Cathy graduated from high school. I became friends with Flora and Andy. I often babysat David. I also babysat Lisa MR who lived in the apartment building next to the rectory. Flora was a voice of reason in my life. We had some long conversations about love and life. I'd started seeing a young man named Carlisle and fell madly in love. He had a violent temper, and I thought my love could change that. Flora counselled me otherwise. There was no way that my love could change anyone else. Only me.

I was strangely attracted to Carlisle because he exhibited a part of me that I had closed off completely—my anger. I still have the scar on my right leg just below my knee where he caught me with a knife. He used to throw things and have other temper outbursts. It was exhilarating. It was terrifying. He joined the army and was training to be a cook.

He really wanted to go to Vietnam. I was desperate to keep him home. His mom and I talked about ways we could do this but to no avail. Tragically, he became one of the many to succumb to that vicious war. My heart was broken. My fiancé was dead. The losses in my life were mounting up.

The last year of high school, my work experience was at Burlin Photo Studios on 6th Street in New Westminster. I took some photos of the people who worked at the studio and was given some instruction on lighting and composition. I still have the proofs that were taken of me by the owner of the company. I had a real passion for photography.

I also compiled my first book of poetry and short stories that year. I created the cover and put a photo of my 'mug' there. There were several dozen poems in it, all of which I had written during those high school years.

In March 1968, I moved back home with mom. My foster mother and I had come to a mutual agreement that I would go back home before we both killed each other. I was delighted. I'm sure she was relieved, too.

It was so comfortable to be with my mom and siblings again even though she was dating a real nut case named Art. He was mean, and we were all scared of him. I don't know what she saw in him. But I was drinking almost daily by that time, and I was smoking like a chimney so who was I to think like that?

While I was in foster care, my mom went to Business College in an effort to improve herself and her living conditions. She was hired as a bookkeeper with Phelps' Moving and Cartage. I was so proud of her accomplishments. She never let life get her down for long. She was a real role model for me.

My family and I knew how to have a good time on a budget. We played *Charades* and *Twister*. We enjoyed hot chocolate and cinnamon toast for a snack. Then we'd all get up and jive together. The furniture got pushed back and we'd dance the night away. Mom was always ready to party, without benefit of booze, and we had some rockin' times at our house.

I include here a piece I wrote in 1968 about a typical morning in our house. My mom loved it so much that she typed out a copy for each of us. Then she matted it with red and white gingham checks and framed it with a glass front. I appreciated her efforts and her silent message to me of, "Well, done, daughter."

"Early Morning Rut"

"Pull-up. Rise. Roll over and open your tightly closed eyes. "Oh, my goodness. It's five to eight. Lynnette, arouse. Dash up and wake up the girls." Drowsy, sleepy slumber… I succeed in erecting my body to a sitting position.

Switch on the light – turn up the heat – put the kettle on for tea. Run up the stairs – trip at the top and stub my toe. Into the bedroom – TALK at the 'kids', "Wake up you lazy sleepy bones. C'mon, Claire. Hey, Joel. All right now Catharine, Sasha and Victoria. It's eight o'clock."

Down the stairs – grab that damn kettle – turn it off – make the tea – put in the toast – turn the heat on under the cast iron frying pan.

Egg-timer ding. Egg timer off. Toaster pop. Toast buttered.

Silence? No. THUD … three teenage girls, an eleven-year old boy, and a seven-year old girl come crashing down the rickety old staircase.

"Sit down and eat your breakfast. You've got five minutes 'til the bus comes!"

Five screaming kids and a frustrated Mother surround the poor kitchen table.

"THE BUS!" Grab books – grab lunch – grab coat – kiss mom – out the door – up the hill – into the bus –

"Hi, Lois."

Whew!"

Life seemed normal at times, and then the wheels would fall off again. I was dating another young man whose name I can't recall. One day we went to have lunch at his house with his parents. After lunch, he said he had to go buy some cigarettes. I had been smoking for several years by this time. I asked him to pick up a pack for me, as well.

Almost as soon as he was out the door, his folks asked me to come and look at something. They were in their room. They pushed me to the floor and raped me. They described in detail what they were doing to me and what reaction this was having on them. I screamed but that was soon cut off by something else going in my mouth. I was horrified. I was inexperienced sexually though I had done some dating.

I remember there was a white wall on my left and I was lying on a dark wood floor. I recall looking over at the mound of white sheets on top of their bed and thinking that they hadn't made their bed yet, and it was late afternoon. Afterward, they told me if I ever told anyone, they would kill me. I never told until I was in counselling years later in my early thirties.

I started to drink in earnest and was always looking for a way off the planet. My lifestyle went from bad to worse. I felt filthy, unworthy, and unlovable. I tried suicide twice more with booze and drugs. I couldn't even do that right. My thoughts and behaviour showed anyone who had eyes that I had moved as far away from my inner spirit and my higher power as I could get.

I had my own band by that time and we were playing around town. On grad night, I was playing for the opening of La Gardenia Supper Club in Sapperton. I was seventeen not twenty-one but I had falsified my ID to say that I was of age.

I really liked the lead guitar player and had seen him a few times. One night he told me he could never see me again because he had reconciled with his wife. I didn't even know he was married. I was so angry and frustrated by the accumulation of losses to that point in my life that I screamed and swore at him at the top of my lungs. When I left the building, I hit the telephone pole using my fist. I felt like a volcano was going to spew forth from inside of me. The only cure for that was booze. I proceeded to get very drunk.

Booze was my universal wrench. It worked on everything. The joy of it was, that it didn't take a lot to get the job done. But I was a blackout drinker. After a couple of drinks, I have no memory of what went on. I found myself in all kinds of dicey situations where a nice girl should never have been. I was out of control but had years of this behaviour ahead of me.

With three teenage girls close in age, you can imagine the dating that went on in our house. There are a couple of guys that come to mind, who dated most of us. Gary Grant is one of the most memorable. I think he broke all of our hearts. Johnny Isaacs drove a motorcycle and that drove Mom crazy. We all loved the speed and danger as he tore down suicide hill in New Westminster. It was a thrill.

Cyril Blacke was almost a member of our family. He and I dated for a while. He also dated Victoria and Sasha. One time, in the middle of the night, he tried to climb up the drainpipe to see one of us. Of course, this flimsy pipe couldn't begin to hold his six foot plus frame, and he fell back into the rose bushes. It was a real thorny issue... or is that a 'horny' issue?

Amidst all this dating, I was working and earning my own money. I sold both Avon and Vanda Beauty products door to door in my neighbourhood. I also worked at Eaton's in the linens department. Consequently, when I did finally get married, I had a very full Hope Chest—a medium blue trunk with all kinds of treasures in it. I'd managed to squirrel away tea towels and bath linen, a set of dishes, cutlery, pots and pans, all kinds of kitchen gadgets, a wedding book, a baby book, set of sheets, set of three clear glass Pyrex bowls, which I still have today, some fifty years later.

In June 1969, Art, the man my mom was seeing, gave me a beer. I'd never tried a beer before. I drank it back. It was gross. I was heading out with Cyril. He said I could drive. I got behind the wheel. It was a standard stick shift, and he was going to show me what to do. I was trying to go forward down the hill but the car seemed to be stuck.

Art came across the road and started to yell that I didn't know what I was doing. He said I needed to back up before I could go forward. I didn't understand that Cyril had turned the wheels into the curb. I got mad at Art and started going down Alberta Street. I didn't want to go on Columbia because I didn't have my licence and had never had any formal training. I decided to turn right and go behind the graveyard.

The next thing I know, Cyril is yelling, "The brake! Hit the @#$% brake!" I'd blacked out and had not turned the wheel far enough. We smacked into the corner of a house and set it three inches off its foundation, after ripping up twenty foot of fencing and grazing a telephone pole. Usually, there was a child sleeping on the couch on the other side of the wall I hit. Fortunately, the child was sick and sleeping in his bedroom. I was a month away from my eighteenth birthday, so Cyril had to take the brunt of my mistake. My solution – never to drink beer again.

I loved vodka and orange juice and I found it easy to sneak around and have a few as the need arose.

The disease progressed and I became a lone drinker. I looked for opportunities to be alone so I could drink. My food addiction had been firmly supplanted by alcohol. I was not a party girl anymore. I started to lose weight as the alcoholism took over. Where would it end?

Man's first step on the moon was lost in the shuffle of planning and attending my grandparents' sixtieth wedding anniversary in July 1969. It was a gala event at the Sapperton Hall, attended by all but one of their children, my dad. I knew this was a sore spot for both of them, so nothing was mentioned. We hoped he would come. But he was true to form and stayed away. It was encouraging to see these two people together after six decades; an excellent lesson for me—love *can* last a lifetime.

My cousin, Dorothy-Jean, and I sang, "The Anniversary Waltz" as Grandma and Grandpa MacKay danced. The food was yummy, and we had all put on our best 'bib and tucker' to celebrate the occasion.

I met a man named Butch. There was something different about him. He was magnetic to me, I was so attracted to him. We danced all night and I didn't want to let go of him. I told Mom I wanted to go live with him in the states. I couldn't understand why my mom didn't want me to go. I was eighteen, and I had a mind of my own. I thought I was so grown up because I was living in a little walk-up flat on Cornwall Street. I didn't need her permission to live my life the way I wanted. So, I just left without her blessing.

A few nights after I arrived in Seattle, we decided to get married. On our 'wedding night', he beat the hell out of me. He put his boots to my back as I fell to the floor. I was in severe trouble, and I knew it. I lay there for hours bruised, bleeding, and being berated. I was trying to think of what to do. I slowly developed a plan.

Unbeknownst to me, he was a speed freak and had gone out to get more dope. He wanted me to do it but I was terrified of drugs. I had no idea what they would do to me. I was satisfied using alcohol. He became enraged, and I knew that it was only a matter of time before he would come after me again. I stole some money from his mother's wallet and bided my time.

When he unlocked the door to our room the next night, I threw myself at him and pummelled him with my fists. I kicked him with my feet. I got him a good one in the groin and got out of there fast.

I could hear him howling as I ran out of the house. I hid by the garage and kept moving out of sight for a long time. Eventually his want for pills was more urgent than his want to hurt me. He went back into the house. I made my way to the bus depot and bought a ticket home.

I told mom what happened and she had the marriage annulled. It had not been consummated, as, after we married, he was more interested in beating me than making love to me.

Ages thirteen to seventeen had shown me just how bad life could get. Yet, I'd learned nothing about growing up and taking responsibility for my actions. I was forcing my will into all kinds of dangerous situations. I didn't care about myself and what was to come of me. I was careening down a mountain pass with no brakes. No one knew, least of all me, what would happen. I was on a course of self-destruction.

ON THE ROAD AGAIN

I had been working at the Dominion Glass Factory when their union went on strike. I moved back home with mom and the kids and I found another job in the linen department of the Eaton's store in downtown New Westminster.

It was the first time in ten years that I had not been actively involved in music. I wasn't writing either. My addiction to alcohol had usurped my desire to be creative. I was eighteen and hanging out at Legions around Vancouver. They were open in the afternoon so I had a lot more drinking time even though I didn't need it.

Saturday, October 4, 1969, I was at the Legion with a girlfriend. My hair was still in rollers. We were nursing a drink, as usual. The band started to play. They were really good so I paid attention. My girlfriend leaned over and said, "Isn't that Sandy a dream boat!" I said that he was, indeed. He was tall with dark hair and a powerful voice. Musicians were my weakness. I heard he was going to be going on tour to Alaska and I made up my mind that I was going with him.

I didn't know what love was, but I was sure I could love this guy and we could make beautiful music together.

I engaged him in conversation when he was on a break. He invited me to the Legion in New Westminster to try out in the talent contest he was playing. I said I'd see him there.

The following Thursday, October 9th, I showed up on time, dressed to the hilt and smelling like a rose. I didn't drink that day because I wanted to make a good impression. I did. Though I didn't win the contest, I won his heart.

He invited me to have Thanksgiving dinner with a few members of his family. On October 12th, he picked me up at two in the afternoon and had a wonderful time with his sister and her family, plus his youngest brother.

We saw each other every day for twenty-two days straight and decided it would be a swell idea to get married. I found out he wasn't Sandy Marino from Sorrento, rather he was Elvin Saulson from Salmon Arm. He was a schoolteacher by trade. I loved his name because it sounded classy. I couldn't wait to be Mrs. E. Saulson. I wrote it over and over on every piece of paper available.

My sister, Victoria, and I started to plan the wedding. We had no money and only one month to pull it off. Mom really liked El but was dubious about our match because of the age difference. He was thirty-four, and I was eighteen.

The day after we announced our engagement, El flew to Fairbanks, Alaska, to begin the gig with The Mike Harris Band.

Mike Harris was an extraordinary fiddle player. His rendition of "The Orange Blossom Special" left no one in their seat. He played his instrument above his head, between his legs, and behind his back. Mike was a mover and a shaker. He knew how to get the job done. So did El. Though they respected each other, there was always this feeling of tension between them.

Gracie Dee was Mike's wife. She had a voice that rivalled Tammy Wynette's. Her forceful personality and high energy shone through as she belted out song after song with nary a breath in between. They were an exciting duo, and I learned a lot about what it took to put on an intense show.

This was no ordinary audience. The guys had come down from the DEW (distant early warning) line for a good time. They were loud, boisterous, and quite obviously horny. Most of them wore guns that were sometimes brandished about. The week before I arrived in Alaska, there were three murders and several rapes. There was very little law established in this frontier land.

Meanwhile, Victoria and I were at home getting our job done, too. She was handling the catering and hosted a bridal shower for me. She and Flora Pilas were to be my Maid and Matron of Honour. Claire was my flower girl. El's brothers, Lou and Justin were his best man and usher respectively. We visited with El's sister, Marni, and put together a guest list. Then she put on a shower for me with El's side of the family. At the shower, El's Mom, Nana, sat beside me. She said, "You'll never be good enough for my son. By the way, you're not the first girl to wear that engagement ring." I responded, "What do you mean?" She replied that El had been engaged in the summer to another woman then she broke it off. He gave me the same ring and never told me. To this day, he doesn't know that I know this. This short conversation foreshadowed an eight-year relationship fraught with lies and half-truths.

Victoria and I mailed out a hundred invitations purchased from the Jackson Printing Company in New Westminster. We ordered the bouquets and boutonnières of red roses. Mom ordered the wedding cake from my second cousin Evelyn's husband, Greig Walker. We found such items as the garter belt, the Bride and Groom goblets, the cake-cutting knife, and the Wedding Album. Our neighbour, Joyce volunteered to do our hair, and she loaned me her wedding dress.

Someone else produced a veil. El's uncle, Gordon McLaren (his dad's twin brother) agreed to perform the ceremony at the United Church on Franklin Street in Vancouver.

The wedding night was booked at the Airport Inn. It was all coming together. People were really pleasant and giving. Though the weather was stormy, in the end, we had a perfect wedding day.

There were two receptions; one at mom's, for my side of the family, and one at Marni's in Surrey, for El's side of the family. This was very disappointing as the families never did come together under one roof. There just wasn't enough time to book a hall and no one had a home large enough to accommodate all of the guests. Nana, true to nature, had another slight for me. She sat on the arm of my chair and, without even giving me a glance she said, "You're not the woman for my son. He'll never really love you." I felt defeated.

I had chosen a cream coloured coatdress with a faux leopard collar and cuffs for my going away outfit. It was perfect on my five foot two, one hundred and eight pound frame. While I was changing, Victoria burst into the room, almost in tears. She said another woman was wearing the same outfit I had on. I told her not to worry about it. Everyone knew I was the bride. As I came down the stairs, I spotted the lady. It was El's cousin. She was about the same size as I was, with similar colouring, and she looked just as good as I did. I walked over to her and said, "You have a good fashion sense. You look fabulous!"

"So do you," she agreed as we hugged. This put everyone at ease and we went on with the reception.

People had heard that El and I were going to tour Alaska. We received thirteen blankets, all of which we had to leave in storage at Mom's. We also received a number of serving trays for some reason that has escaped me for all these years. This wouldn't happen today as gift giving is made so easy using the Bridal Registry at most of the larger department stores.

I had had way too much vodka and was feeling very tipsy. I don't remember if El and I actually got around to, well, you know … We'd had such a busy two days and then, after the reception at Mom's, we had to drive downtown to Vancouver to get a new fiddle bow for Mike from his friend's house. It was in the wee hours when we made our way out to Richmond and into our honeymoon suite.

The next thing I remember is El standing across the room wearing only his white under shorts. He was on the phone, thanking someone for waking us up. I was very foggy-headed and thought to myself *what have I done, now?*

We got up and ready to go to the airport for a flight aboard Alaska Airlines. The butterflies in my stomach were fluttering away, and I felt quite queasy.

We were heading to Fairbanks. I'd never been on a plane before, and I loved it. It was more than I'd ever imagined. I was mesmerized, gazing out across a field of white clouds punctuated by mountain peaks. I was stunned to see that the sky was so blue above the clouds. It was an up-side-down world. As usual, I took lots of pictures.

El was regaling me with stories of the rapes and murders that had happened in Fairbanks over the last few weeks. The last drummer, also named Sandy, had been shot as he sat playing his drums in the club into which we were booked. El told me about a runner who had died from ice crystals in his lungs. He said a little kid had been licking the ice from a metal door when his tongue got stuck solid and a rescue squad of some sort had been called in. The place was rugged and wild, and he sounded so excited about it all. I was quite nervous.

This was the farthest I had ever been from my mom, and I was wondering about the sanity of my decision to marry El and go to Alaska. It had all sounded quite good in my head. I'd been in other fixes, and they had worked out okay. Maybe this would work out okay, too. I still had my falsified ID, so I ordered some of those tiny little bottles of booze, and we landed safely.

Mike picked us up at the airport. He was in a rush, as they had to get ready for the show. He asked El if he had explained about the two kids I was going to be babysitting. Babysitting! El blanched. He hadn't quite gotten around to telling me that. There was no spot for me in the band because I was underage and not in the Musicians' Union. I was not allowed to sing in the show. I was to be the babysitter for Mike and Gracie's two little kids. I was stunned into silence.

An hour after we were settled into our room at Mike and Gracie's mobile home trailer, El left to go to work while I sat and cried my heart out. It was November 23, 1969, minus forty-two degrees Fahrenheit, and I was alone in a strange country with a head full of horror stories and two little kids to look after. I was heartbroken; not a good way to start a marriage.

A few years before, while I was in foster care, the movie "Psycho" had aired on TV. During a commercial break after the shower scene, I went to get the Reverend his evening cup of Postum. The Mrs. was doing some mending. As I was walking back into the living room, she raised her scissors to me and roared. It frightened me so badly that I dropped the tray and started to cry. She belittled me by telling me I couldn't take a joke. Ever after that, I was not able to take a shower.

Now, with the kids in bed, I wanted to take a soothing bath but there was no plug for the tub. I was forced to take a shower. I went hunting for booze. When I was good and hammered, I had a shower and went to bed awaiting the return of my husband.

Life in Alaska was not what I had imagined. It was dark most of the time, and it was really cold. I was lonely for my family. I talked to mom and my siblings once a week from wherever we were.

I was a NEWS junky and was constantly being scared out of my wits by what was happening around me in Fairbanks. Outside of the four walls of this tiny three-bedroom trailer, life was rough. People were rowdy and each had their own perception of the law of the land. I never felt safe there, and I couldn't wait to leave.

Though El was making good money, we never seemed to have any. Once a week he would sit down with his cheque book and then go off to the post office with a stack of white envelopes. I had no idea what was going on. I decided to have a serious heart to heart with him. Why we were always broke was beyond me. We were staying rent-free with Mike and Gracie. Did he owe money? Was he in trouble? I came to the stark realization that I knew nothing about him or his past. But I was bound to find out. He was my husband, and I expected him to be forthcoming with me. He told me he was over ten thousand dollars in debt, a huge sum in the 1970s. He explained all the whys and wherefores and, together, we worked out a plan.

I took over the finances and within two years, we were debt free. I was good with money. This was something I didn't know about myself, as I'd never had any before.

While we were still in Fairbanks, I discovered that I was a few months pregnant. We were so excited, we could hardly contain ourselves. It was a few days after Christmas and a Chinook had blown through leaving everything green, warm, and watery. Going outside,

I felt like I had walked into a Monet painting. Everything was going to be okay. We were going to have a baby.

Raising a child was something I knew about, and my confidence in myself as a woman soared. We started talking about baby names and settling down and where we wanted to live.

Then, one day in February, I started spotting. In no time, larger blood clots were being released. Hasty preparations were being made to get me back down to Vancouver. Hospital conditions were somewhat primitive in Fairbanks. I lost the baby, my perfect little boy, in the toilet at the Airport. He was about four or five inches long and translucent. I could see his little veins and penis. There was nothing I could do for him. He was dead. I cried hysterically. I couldn't catch my breath. There was no one to hold me, so I held onto the porcelain toilet. I was hemorrhaging and started to vomit. I cleaned myself up and, in a daze, I went to tell El that we had lost our baby. I felt so guilty. What was wrong with me?

I boarded the plane alone and landed in Vancouver several hours later. I was deeply depressed. Where the first plane ride to Alaska had been an amazing adventure high above the clouds, this trip was dismal, at best.

Mom took me to see her doctor who put me in the hospital and performed a D&C. I waited for my husband to come down a few weeks later.

Not long after that, we drove north on the Alaska Highway heading to Whitehorse. We had a job at the Kopper King up on the hill. A few weeks into it, the house band came back, and we were out of a job again. Sammy Starr, our lead guitarist, got on the phone and found us a gig in Seward, Alaska. All we had to do was get there.

Have you ever tried to get out of Whitehorse in the dead of winter? It may be different today, but back in 1970 it was a challenge. The bus for that week had already been through town. There was no train and no direct flights. We were stuck.

We'd made friends with a man named Ron who owned a four-seater Cherokee piper cub. He offered to fly us to Anchorage where we could catch a bus down the coast. The hitch was only El and I could go along with one amplifier, one microphone, and El's six-string guitar in the plane, which left room for one small bag with our costumes and toiletries. During the flight, I set about learning a variety of songs to compensate for our lack of group members.

Flying in a single engine plane was a horse of a completely different colour. The weather was dicey, and we were grounded at the Alaska border because a robbery had taken place in Fairbanks. The escape had been made in the same type of plane we were flying. We fit the description of the robbers. It was a scary situation.

I had been too long without food and was starting to feel clammy and shaky. El explained that I was hypoglycemic and needed a meal with sugar and protein posthaste. We were at the jailhouse being questioned, and our plea for food was ignored. It wasn't until I lost consciousness and had to be revived with sugar water, that they produced a steak dinner and all the trimmings from a restaurant next door.

There was some problem with the flight plan that Ron had filed, and this is what had detained us. Ron kept telling the licence number to the border patrol and, for some reason, they didn't understand it. There was a zed at the end and that just didn't compute. After a few back and forths, the guard said, "Oh, you mean zee!" Ron chuckled and said "Yes, but Canadians pronounce the last letter of the alphabet as Zed", and Zee is something you wipe your ass with. Everyone was laughing by that time. In the end, we continued our journey with fond farewells and many apologies from them for the inconvenience.

We were headed for Anchorage but it was socked in, so we had to divert our flight to Fairbanks. This was not good as we were very low on fuel. We barely made it in. But, I guess that's all we needed to do.

We booked a flight out of Fairbanks to Anchorage. We then boarded a 'bus', which was really a long van carrying seven other people, their suitcases, and their dogs. Off we drove down the Alaskan coast. It was a frightening trip. The driver was a maniac, and the road left much to be desired.

Seward was a few blocks long and a few more wide. There was one greasy spoon, several bars, one of which sold food, and a variety store with a sandwich counter. We ate all of our meals at the variety store. It was clean and smelled good, my criteria for almost everything.

Someone had found us a drummer. Drummers are a unique group of individuals who march to their own beat, so to speak. Anyone who is a musician and is reading this will get my meaning, unless, of course, they're a drummer. We never had much luck with drummers but if you can get a good one, there's nothing like it. This particular drummer could not beat his way out of a paper bag. Half way through the night, we thanked him and he was excused. The folks just weren't that drunk. Luckily, I'd brought along my tambourine and that's what kept the beat.

We had fun on that gig, just El and I. We developed some really tight duets and practised for hours so we could put on a good show. This was really important to both of us. It didn't go unappreciated. We performed songs by George Jones and Tammy Wynette, Porter Wagoner and Dolly Parton, and Loretta Lynn and Conway Twitty. Word got around that the country-singing duo of "Sandy Marino and Lyndi-Lou" were in town. Over the next few weeks, the audience swelled from a few to several dozen. Sometime later, Sammy Starr called to say he had found us another job in Anchorage, and we were off again.

We took the bus back up the coast and settled in a motel close to the club. I loved singing with El. Our voices blended so nicely, and I loved being with him. Aside from our music, we were both interested in UFO's and the possibility of life on other planets. We enjoyed playing *Cribbage* and *Scrabble*, and taking long walks. Our marriage was settling down into a comfortable routine. I really needed that.

I suspected I was pregnant again. We came out of our doldrums and started to make big plans for this new addition to our family. Then, one sunny morning in early June, I woke up with severe cramps and heavy bleeding. El took me to emergency. It was discovered through an ultrasound that I had an ectopic pregnancy. Without any further ado, they relieved me of my baby, our second little boy. There was no time for anesthetic. Did you know there are one-hundred and twenty-eight black marks on acoustic ceiling tiles? I used counted numbers against the pain.

I didn't think I would be able to go on. I was warned to take it easy and back off from lovemaking for at least six to eight weeks. I brought out my old pal, alcohol, and got good and drunk. The baby was never mentioned again. Life goes on, I was told. Didn't anyone think I knew that at this point in my life?

When our contract was over, we moved back down to Vancouver and into a motel on Canada Way. We got a gig on Hastings Street. A few weeks later, an opportunity to go to Vietnam presented itself. We had arranged our passports and were in the process of getting our shots updated. There was a sign at the table where we went to get our next shots, which said something like 'If you suspect you are pregnant please refrain from taking this shot'. I suspected I was pregnant. I know the doctor had said to wait six to eight weeks but, well, you know… We weren't able to go to Vietnam to entertain the troops.

We were on our way to Alaska for our third tour. I was trying to put the past behind me. We hadn't even been married for a year and already there were some deep scars on our relationship. I was determined to make my marriage work and pull myself out of this horrible pit I was in. I didn't know what it would take to get me out, but I was willing.

Country music is such a personal experience for many people. I poured my heart into my songs. I plumbed the depths of my personal recent experience and used it to add new dimensions to my singing. My music was a panacea for my wounded heart. It was working. I began to feel lighter.

On a warm day in August, I felt that little fluttering again. I was pregnant. In the early days of our marriage, I was never able manage the six to eight weeks of abstinence that the doctor was always harping about. I took after my mom too much in that area.

We were walking down a street in Anchorage and could see a towering mountain in the vista ahead of us. We were holding hands and talking a mile a minute. We came upon a jewellery store and went in to have a look. El bought me an Alaska gold nugget and diamond watchband set with a point eighty-seven karat diamond on either shoulder. It was absolutely stunning. We knew that, with a child on the way, there wouldn't be much opportunity to buy such luxury items in the future. It became a symbol of our inner wealth. We counted our blessings.

We finished our job there and went back home to the coast where we settled in Vancouver. We were living on the main floor of a furnished house at 453 East 10th Avenue. El got a job as a substitute teacher and I started a booking agency to book bands from the States into local clubs.

By the time our first anniversary came around on the November 22, 1970, I was well into my third pregnancy. We had done three tours to Alaska and one to Whitehorse. I was just nineteen years old.

A MOMMY, AT LAST

Our child was due to be born at the end of February 1971. On the twenty-eighth day, I was admitted into Grace Hospital in Vancouver. We were excited. The anticipation had been mounting since we had passed that critical four-month period where we had lost our two other little boys.

The labour pains came closer. Mom was coaching me on my breathing. I repaid her by squeezing her wedding rings into her fingers, almost drawing blood. She was patient and understanding. She was no stranger to this situation, and it was comforting to have her close by.

The contractions were down to two minutes apart and the nurses were prepping me for delivery when, without warning, everything stopped. After several hours with no further activity, I was sent home to wait.

I'm not one to be able to sit on my duff. I booked more gigs then played and sang as usual. My belly was all out in front, so while I was facing the audience, no one could tell I was expecting. However, when I turned to have a sip of water, my secret was out, and I could hear the audience tittering.

For months, I had pined for my baby. I would go into our room and stand over the crib. It was waiting. I poured over the tiny outfits in the dresser drawers. I was waiting. I had spent most of my life, waiting. The doctors said they could induce, but it was my belief that this child had a date in mind, and I was bound to stick it out and see what that was going to be.

On April 15, 1971 at 10:59 p.m. I watched as our son, Daniel, was born. It was an extra-long pregnancy, but he was worth waiting for. El was playing that night, and it was way past my mom's bedtime, so I was on my own. His red head poked its way out and then with one giant push, came out in a gush. "It's a boy!" exclaimed the doctor. I was thrilled. As I looked into those piercing blue eyes, it was El's face staring back at me. The first words I said to this new little person were, "You are your father's child." I was so moved that I started to cry. I was ecstatic and completely enchanted by this new human being. I was in love. He was a healthy seven pounds ten ounces with all his fingers and toes.

They cleaned and stitched me up and I waited in the hall as my room was being readied. El came at 1:30 a.m. I was so proud to be able to say to him, "We have a son."

A few hours later, they brought Daniel to me and showed me how to nurse. This was no easy task. Everyone said it was so natural. In reality, it is a learned skill. I became adept over the next few weeks, as most of us do.

Back then, women were kept in the hospital for several days and taught how to change, bathe, dress, and feed their baby. I stayed at Grace Hospital for five days. The day we brought Daniel home was the most miraculous day of my life. I was ready to be a Mom. I had all this love inside me to pour out on him. I had strong ideas about how I wanted him raised and what I wanted to teach him.

My dream for my son was that he would always know that he was loved for himself. If he should show any inclination to do this or that, we would support him whole-heartedly. We hoped he would live his life with passion and compassion, would find a love to last and sustain him through the joys and trials of life, and would be able to give that same kind of love to another. We had big dreams for our little boy.

During my pregnancy, I had slowed down on the drinking and was feeling somewhat healthier. We still had the band and the booking agency. We made a decision to discontinue with the latter. I wanted to be with Daniel and sing and that was it. It was getting closer to the end of the school year and El didn't have another teaching job for the following September. We decided to move. I was expecting again, and he needed a full time position to support his growing family.

The day that Daniel turned three months, we headed up the Fraser Canyon to Falkland. El had gotten a teaching position. He said he wanted to stop by and see his parents in Blind Bay, some forty-five miles out of our way. When we got to Blind Bay, I found out that we weren't going to Falkland until September, the start of the school year. We were going to be staying in Blind Bay with his mom and dad for the next two months. I was getting fed up with El skirting around issues he didn't want to deal with head on. He knew what my response would be to staying with his parents and that's why he didn't bother to tell me. His lying was breaking my heart and wearing away at our marriage.

Nana (El's mother) and I had not gotten off to a good start. She made it clear that she didn't support our getting married, and I should give it a good hard think. I did. I thought she was a downright *(well, you know)*.

Still, she was El's mom, so I tried to make a go of it. It really bothered me when people didn't like me, so I worked hard at being a good wife, mother, and homemaker to try and earn her approval. It never happened, even to this day, thirty-two years later.

El and Papa built a tool shed close to the water's edge of the Shuswap Lake and the three of us moved in there at the end of July. Nana and I had some nasty fights. Papa always stuck up for me and then Nana would go into a sulk.

There were forest fires everywhere, and El decided he would go and put out a few. He left a few days after his birthday on the fourth of August. I lost our baby a week later. I spent a couple of days in hospital in Salmon Arm. When I came back to Blind Bay, Nana had completely taken over my position as Daniel's mother. I couldn't wait to leave. I was so worried about El and hoped he would be home soon.

He was gone for almost a month. I wrote to him, but I never mentioned losing the baby. He was in danger, and I didn't want to have him worrying about me, too. On Labour Day we packed up our few belongings and moved into a furnished motel suite in Falkland, thirty miles from Salmon Arm. The space had a kitchen, living room, bedroom, and bathroom. It was really a comfortable place and quite scenic. The best thing of all was that Nana was nowhere in sight.

While El was teaching, I set out with Daniel exploring the neighbourhood. I made friends with the townspeople and had visits with some of the shopkeepers. We went for long walks. The heat always did me in. I found it difficult to get around because my legs sometimes felt so tired in hot weather; like I was walking through Jell O. Autumn was always my favourite time of the year. I loved the crunch and the colours, the sun and the cool air and being able to have more energy.

In short order, I discovered that I was pregnant, yet again. The doctor said I should stay in bed and rest. I asked him if he had any suggestions on how to care for a six-month old baby from one's bed. He had no answer for me, so I just carried on. A few months later, I lost my fourth little boy.

I wasn't a daily drinker, I was a binge drinker, and when I couldn't deal with something, I drank. I knew I was a good mother, but I kept losing my babies. What was I doing wrong? This question haunted me, and I started to analyse my behaviour in earnest. I became a perfectionist and a clean freak. I thought it was germs or something like that, so I bathed several times a day in Detol and very hot water. This dried out my skin and gave me an antiseptic odour. Solution–slather on more perfume.

I became so nuts about cleanliness and orderliness that, upon awakening from a nap one day, I noticed that the green tissues covering the Christmas oranges were wrinkled. I got up and ironed them. I could also be found in the middle of the night down on my knees with a brush trying to pick up undetectable lint from the carpet.

I was doing my best to control my outside world so these things would stop happening. Meanwhile, the chaos within me raged.

I went to the doctor, and he gave me a complete physical. I was sent for a test in Kamloops, and it was discovered that I had endometrial cancer.

I can still see El, backlit from the hospital hall light, all six foot two of him filling the doorway, as he tentatively entered my room. He had been crying. We both wanted another child. We wanted a daughter, if at all possible. We discussed it for over an hour. I made the decision that we would try one more time, putting off treatment for a while. The doctor was aghast. What were we thinking?

Our risk paid off. Almost immediately, I became pregnant with our daughter Darlene. She was delivered breech on the October 11, 1972 at 4:53 p.m., after seventy-four hours of labour. They tried to turn her but it didn't work. I recall the doctor coming into the room and asking me what I thought I was doing. I told him I was doing the deep breathing exercises I had learned from Kareen's Yoga, a television program I always watched and did each time it was on. Yoga was one of the tools I used the most to get through the stresses of my life back then. He told me to forget it and just scream like the rest of the women. I told him to get out!

Darlene was a perfectly formed little bundle with blue eyes and a frothy mound of black hair on her head. She was a little bigger than her brother, weighing in at eight pounds ten ounces. The length of her foot was the same as my middle finger. My first words to her were "You're a miracle, my daughter." Of course, I realize that Daniel is just as much a miracle. He made it, against the odds, and with me losing four other little boys.

Darlene was a howler and made it known when she wasn't being fed fast enough or changed soon enough. Babies are little emotional sponges. It was more than likely that she was picking up on my stress over my physical health.

I was able to nurse her for a few months before I underwent surgery and chemotherapy in March 1973. By that point, the cancer had spread so my uterus, cervix and an inch of my vagina were removed. I was only twenty-one and already at the end of my childbearing years. But, we had our two lovely children, our little miracles, and even though I wanted a houseful like my mom, this would have to be enough for me.

We had moved out of Falkland to the family home in Notch Hill just before Darlene was born. It was an old house to which El had been brought home as a baby some thirty-seven years before. Nana and Papa had rented it to us for a fair price. We were fifteen miles from Salmon Arm and a mile and a half up the hill from Sorrento. I didn't drive. After the incident where I put the car into a house, I'd lost my nerve. I felt isolated.

One day I heard a knock at the door. There were two Jehovah's Witnesses at the door. I was canning green tomato mincemeat and there were quart jars all over the table and counters. The aroma of Christmas was in the air on this hot June day. Though I was always busy, I was very lonely and starving for some adult conversation. El was teaching at Carlin School. He left at 7:00 in the morning and, after coaching the girls' soccer team, too, he didn't get home until after 6:00 at night. Then after supper we had bath-time, stories, and bedtime before we had a chance to talk. But then he had to mark papers and prepare exams. It seemed like we never had any time just for us. I missed him.

The Jehovah's Witness ladies came out once a week. We did Bible study in my kitchen for several months. El didn't approve. His spiritual platform was, "There are four hundred and sixty-six different sects to the Christian religion. Why is my interpretation wrong?" Except for marriages, funerals, and christenings, we were never in a church together. I went alone. I was always a spiritual seeker.

I had a real problem with the possibility of never being able to celebrate birthdays and Christmases again. The dogma of the Witnesses' religion stated that these celebrations were pagan. But they were an institution in my family. I decided to break my connection with these two helpful ladies. There was not even any point in maintaining a friendship. They were more different than I chose to be. I went back to St. Mary's Anglican Church at the bottom of the hill in Sorrento.

When the kids were toddlers, I called Daniel 'my little sunshine boy', Darlene was somewhat moody and unpredictable. She was also extremely creative. They were active all day long. It was a lot of fun to be with them with their goofy sense of humour. We laughed a lot. They'd be playing quietly with *Lego* in the living room then all of a sudden bang into the back of me, their little arms wrapped tight around my knees. "I love you, Mommy."

I loved to read to them. The bedtime routine was my favourite as we slowly calmed down after supper and relaxed into bath time then reading. I often sat on the edge of their beds after they'd gone to sleep, so grateful for a chance to be their mom.

El and I played at little halls in the interior of British Columbia: Carlin, Glen Eden, Sorrento, Celista, Salmon Arm, Adams River, Scotch Creek, and Anglemont to name a few. I loved to entertain, sing, dance, and be with other people. It was the one level on which we shared as equals. We were a real team on stage. Our duets were renowned and requested each time we played. Being creative in this way came naturally to me. I cut my teeth on country music, on the stage, and on the road.

The most fun I had, as an entertainer, was the Battle of the Bands at the Armstrong Fair in the mid-seventies. Three country/rock bands were booked into the arena on the Saturday night. One of us would kick off a rocker like, "S-A-T-U-R-D-A-Y-Night" by the Bay City Rollers. The next band would join in and finally the third one. Each group would try to outdo the other ones with fancy licks or drum solos. Some songs would last for fifteen or twenty minutes. The crowd would go wild, and who can resist that. That is what fed the hole in me—applause and smiling faces.

Except for several songs, I hadn't written a word since the day we were married. I was busy creating in other ways: raising our kids, indoor gardening, cooking, canning, pottery, bowling, liquid embroidery, and keeping the house. We still had the band 'Sandy Marino and

The Sandmen featuring Lindy-Lou' (that was me). We usually had a gig on Friday and Saturday evening, with a rehearsal one night a week. I was also bowling twice a week. El was busy with his responsibilities at school. Though my life seemed full, there was something missing. I sometimes felt I was just going through the motions.

One Sunday, I returned home from church to find Daniel playing on the kitchen floor with my best China teapot. His dad was passed out cold on the bathroom floor. El didn't drink alcohol. I didn't know what was wrong with him. I called the babysitter who, having been in the tub, rushed down the lane with her hair still in a towel. I didn't have my drivers' licence. Nevertheless, we packed him into the car, and I took off.

On the straight stretch before the hill and Carlin School, I noticed I was doing over ninety miles an hour. Then I noticed a cop car up ahead. He was flagging me down. I pulled over to the side. He asked for my licence. I told him I didn't have one. He could see El beside me. I quickly explained that I had found him on the floor and didn't know what had happened. He said, "Follow me!" He ran and jumped back in his car. With sirens blaring and lights flashing, we sped into Salmon Arm and to the Shuswap Lake General Hospital.

El's appendix had burst. He was very lucky that he didn't die right on the spot. Papa and Nana came to the hospital with Keary and Gail, some friends of ours from Blind Bay. Keary drove our '66 Galaxy 500 home while I waited with El's parents to hear the news.

The doctor came out and told us what a close call it had been. The tension of the whole situation made me start to laugh with the relief. Nana thought I was being cruel. She said she knew I never loved El the way she did and that if I did, I would have been crying not laughing.

This proved it all to her. I was an evil person. She hadn't stopped to think I had just saved El's life and was terrified of losing him.

We were told that he would be in the hospital for several weeks with a drainage tube to prevent infection. At that time, teachers were paid once a month for the ten-month school year. We always divided El's annual earnings by twelve instead of ten so we would be okay during this long break. Two months of summer break were upon us.

I told Papa that I needed to learn how to drive right away and asked if he could please teach me. Papa came up to the house every day for a few weeks and gave me driving lessons. Three of his mantras have stayed with me to this day. They are: 'brake into the corner and drive out', 'drive as if you don't have any brakes' and 'don't drive on other people's ability'. All of this was very good advice. He told me I was a good driver and instilled confidence in me.

With Papa beside me, I would drive to and from the hospital every day to see my husband. I took the drivers' test and passed. I had my licence. El and papa were really proud of me. This was a huge and scary step, but it was necessary. I was out in the country with two little kids for several weeks while El was in the hospital. I had to learn to depend on myself now.

El came home eight weeks later, towards the end of summer. I had missed him being home. It just wasn't the same without him. He went back to school a few weeks later.

One day, I was talking on the phone with my best friend, Gail. From my vantage point on a stool by the chimney in the kitchen, I could see all of the kitchen, the short hallway, and part of the kid's bedroom. Darlene, almost one, was sleeping in her playpen. Daniel, almost two and a half, was playing in their room.

The next thing I knew, I could see a double of myself in the middle of the kitchen rolling around on the floor and screaming, "They didn't do that to me. No. No. No! Don't do that to me." The cozy domestic scene was shattered by the emergence of memories of the rape when I was thirteen.

Why I remembered at this particular time in my life is a mystery. How I could have repressed such an outrageous act is even more mysterious. For the next period of time, I ranted and raved and broke up our kitchen. Gail heard it all on the other end of the phone and hung up to call the police and ambulance. She thought someone had broken into our house and was actually raping me. I can only imagine what this must have done to my children. To see their mother like this must have been very traumatizing.

El was called from school. Nana was called to come and look after the kids. I was taken to the psych ward at SLGH and put in restraints. My mind had snapped.

I was there for a few weeks. When I came out, I decided to get good and drunk, as that had always worked for me before. This time the alcohol wouldn't stay down. As soon as it hit my stomach, it flew back out. I could no longer drink. I became depressed.

I was seeing a psychiatrist and he soon noticed I wasn't coming around. He prescribed Valium (diazepam) to relax me, Elavil (amitriptyline) to improve my mood, and T3 painkillers for my body, which had sustained some fairly severe blows from my ordeal in the kitchen. I had always been afraid of drugs and had never tried anything except alcohol. But I loved my husband and kids. I knew I had to get better.

I did start to come out of it. Over a couple of weeks, the fog lifted and I returned home to my kids, the band, and a fairly normal life.

Tropical plants–green and alive–became a huge hobby for me. I made friends with the woman who ran the flower shop. She was very easy to talk to. I bought every tropical she sold over the course of the next few years. I also invested in some books about their care. In the end, I learned the Latin binomials and could say and identify them easily in others' homes. We ended up with seventy-six gorgeous plants. El didn't mind at all, except on watering day.

I became captain of a bowling team and really enjoyed the experience. The kids were in gymnastics and loved it. I loved being their mom. I did the usual motherly things like taking them to swimming classes, to Canoe beach to swim, and on picnics. Some of my friends had kids the same age as mine so we coffee-klatched with them, at times. We alternately spent the holidays with my family at the coast and El's family in Salmon Arm.

I was recognized around town and enjoyed the little bit of notoriety. The band was going strong and we were always working, being requested to do the same gigs year after year.

Alcohol was not working for me any more so over the next couple of years, I learned how to abuse pills. I would lie and say that I had accidentally dropped the bottle into the toilet or down the sink and needed more or some other transparent excuse. I learned how to be really sneaky and crafty in order to get more pills. When I overdid it, I was taken to the hospital and put on psyche ward again. I tried to commit suicide a few times during those years. It wasn't that El and the kids were not good enough. It was that I was not good enough to live. I was damaged beyond repair. In my mind, if I'd been worthy of love, the rapes would not have happened to me. Why didn't someone do something about it at the time? I was a child who went un-noticed.

El and I alternately filled a hospital bed—he with nine hernia repairs and me with cancer, depression, alcoholism, and prescription drug addiction.

Around my twenty-fourth birthday, I woke up with the left side of my face and head in agony. I thought it was my teeth. I went to the dentist who sent me to my doctor who sent me to a neurologist who diagnosed me with trigeminal neuralgia. This is a painful inflammation and/or infection of the three nerves on one side of the face. I felt like molten lead was being poured over my face and pulling it down. I screamed in pain. I also had a cold sore on the lower left lip. El was always getting them and it was thought that I contracted it that way. The cold sore is an infection caused by herpes simplex virus and it sometimes infects the nerve, I was told. This situation lasted for nine days until the carbamazepine that I'd been prescribed kicked in. I couldn't eat or talk or think or wash my hair. I was a zombie with pain and that took up all the space in my head.

It's difficult to describe to a person who has never had the experience. It's hard to fathom that a person could have that kind of pain and live through it. It's called the 'suicide disease' for a reason. Gradually, as the medication worked its miracle, I began to come out of it. From then on, I lived in fear of having another attack.

El and I had ceased our lovemaking after my treatment for cancer a few years before. I don't know why. He just didn't find me attractive or appealing anymore, I suppose. When I approached him for intimacy, he called by a slut or a filthy whore in front of our children. I was completely devastated and demoralized.

We still kissed the odd time. Now, I became obsessed and was always watching him for any sign of a cold sore. A few months later, I had another attack, this time, without the cold sore. I had the virus and there was nothing I could do about it. This attack lasted for sixteen days. Again, the carbamazepine worked its wonders.

The mind is very plastic and always turning towards happiness. It wants to be well. Over time, I forgot about myself and again concentrated on El and the kids.

In August 1977, my sister Sasha, her husband, Ford, and their two kids, Kurt and Jennifer were visiting us from Quesnel. We were at the beach for a swim and Sasha and I had packed up a picnic lunch. Just as we were finishing our feast, a fellow up the beach started crying out, "Elvis is dead. Elvis is dead." The radio said he was found in his home from an apparent overdose of prescription drugs.

He was our fave and now he was gone. My world caved in. I tried to drink again but to no avail. It wouldn't stay down, so there was no point. I just kept popping pill after pill until I was completely oblivious. It was a dark time in my history, one that sometimes haunts me to this day. I continually put my kids in jeopardy by driving while under the influence of prescription drugs. I deliberately use the word prescription to show that a person doesn't have to be on hard drugs or on the streets to hit bottom. By all accounts, I was a young, pretty, talented woman with a husband, two kids, two dogs, two cars, my own home, a fulfilling career, lots of friends and hobbies, and still, I had to get high. I had lost my choice. I was powerless.

One night, I almost fell into the drum set while on stage. The progression of my disease was really starting to show. My private hell was becoming very public and embarrassing to my family. The only difference between my use of alcohol and my use of pills was the effect; I didn't go into a blackout on the drugs. I always remembered everything that I did, to my horror and shame.

Darlene had gone into the hospital because she had a fever again. Bathing her in a tub of cool water would not bring it down. She had been there for a couple of days. I was so out of it I had gone back to bed after El left for work and slept until late afternoon, leaving my six-year old son to fend for himself after school.

At 4:30 p.m. I crawled out of bed and went looking for Darlene. She was nowhere to be found. I gave Daniel a snack. He said, "When are we going to get my sister?" The phone rang and it was the hospital asking me when I was going to pick up my daughter. She had been waiting for me since noon. They had called me in the morning and I had forgotten about her. I jumped in the car with my son and tore off to the hospital.

I walked into the hospital and saw my five-year old daughter sitting on a chair in the waiting room. Her feet were dangling and she was swaying them. She was wearing her powder blue hoodie. All I could see was her profile and blond fringe on her forehead. Her head was bent forward and her demeanour was dejected. I was horrified by what I'd done. My precious girl had been forgotten. I knew how that felt. I knelt before her and deeply apologized.

I signed her out and got a talking to by the doctor. I wanted to rush so we would be there before El got home. I felt completely humiliated, but I was still trying to cover up.

I had been cut-off the drugs the day before because my doctor had received a call from the pharmacy saying I wanted another refill. So, through no virtue of my own, I was forced to go through withdrawals cold turkey. Without a word of an explanation, I went into our room and pushed the dressers against the door. I had no idea what to expect, I just didn't want anyone to see me. El called the doctor who explained what I was going through. The doctor told him to keep me hydrated, if he could.

For a couple of days, I stayed put. I could hear El begging me to come out and go to the hospital. The kids would sit by my door and cry. I felt like I was going to go mad. At that point, I didn't care. I just didn't want to hurt my family anymore.

We had a phone in our bedroom but no phone book. I picked up the receiver and called the local Alcohol and Drug Commission for help. I don't know how I knew what number to call, I just did. It was my first recognizable miracle.

RECOVERING MY SANITY

I sobered up on the October 22, 1977 and have never had to drink or drug since. My first recovery meeting was at an old house on the highway that runs through Salmon Arm. It was called 'The Fireside Group' and was held on a Monday night. I took my first step by admitting I was powerlessness over alcohol and drugs. I vowed to do the remaining eleven perfectly. I thought my perfectionism could really help me to get it right the first time. I fully admitted I'd been out of control.

In January 1978, I went into Aurora House in Vancouver, BC for treatment and was there for twenty-eight days. I discovered that my problem was not alcohol and pills rather my response to life, which was severely askew. My perceptions of reality seemed quite different from those around me. I was far too sensitive and a true people-pleaser, trying to anticipate what those around me wanted then attempting to give it to them immediately. When asked, I had no clue as to what I wanted. My journey towards authenticity was beginning.

In February, my sponsor, Gloria, and I made an appointment to talk with El, make amends for the harm I had done, and see if I could come home. He refused. I think he saw his way out of our marriage. He was certainly justified in taking this position considering what I had put him and our kids through those last few weeks.

Deflated, I stayed in an apartment close by so I could be near my kids. There was no hope of winning my husband's trust again. Having seen him operating in the world for eight years, I knew he didn't forgive easily, if ever. I think he felt it was safer for him to not be in a relationship and he never was again.

Ripe for the picking, I naively had an affair with D-Allan, the director of the recovery house. It had been four years since my husband had touched me and during our last year together he called me a slut and whore in front of the kids anytime I approached him as his wife. D-Allan treated me like a precious queen, and I slurped it up. He and I were together off and on over the next several months.

I had no income and wasn't able to find full-time employment so my friends, Sieg and Louise Silver, took me in. I stayed with them for a few months, healing at Silverglade. I'd met Louise three years prior and taken pottery lessons that were more like life lessons from her. I lived with them twice during that first year of sobriety.

D-Allan and I moved to the coast to be closer to my family as when I would make a date to see the kids, El wouldn't be there. I kept in touch with them by phone and mail.

In July 1978, I called my kids and found out that El had taken off with them. For the next two years, I didn't know where they were. I kept calling the house, and his mother grudgingly told me they were fine but would not tell me where they were. I didn't know if I would ever see them again.

It was Louise Silver who held me together during that time. I called her every few weeks, crying and sick with worry. She counselled and comforted me.

Mom, her new husband, DK, and the rest of the family had established their own lives while I was away for those eight years. A lot of it circled around gambling, drinking, and bars. I just didn't fit in anymore.

I briefly lived with my sister, Catharine, until she decided to move out. Then I was on my own, having permanently broken my ties to D-Allan. I heard a few years later that he'd died in a car crash.

As I was folding laundry one day, some kids yell out 'trick or treat' at my door. I broke down and fell onto the warm clothes sobbing my heart out for my kids. Where were they? Halloween had been an over-the-top event in our home. Each year I worked on their costume and taught them a song to sing. We would then go out in the freezing cold and do our little performance. I loved it and they seemed to, as well. Was El ever going to bring them back? I just didn't know. Maybe he was in another country by now. How long was he going to punish me? He could be very harsh and severe. My dad had fled to the US, and I never saw him again. Was that the fate of me and my kids?

One day, I called the house and El answered the phone. This is a good example of 'there are no accidents or coincidence in life'. I made hasty plans to come up and see my kids.

I flew to Kamloops and Louise picked me up and took me 'home'. We talked long into the night, as was our habit. The next morning, I rented a car and drove up to the house. Nana said they were playing soccer, so I drove back downtown to the park. When we finally connected, he had to point my kids out to me. I hardly recognized them they had grown so much. Daniel was wearing a yellow shirt and playing on the field. Darlene was on the swings behind us. She said to me, "Are you my Mama?" With a lump in my throat, I answered "Yes", and we hugged for a long time. Those few days with my kids were a blessing. I had missed them so. We went out to Silverglade and made some clay pots at Louise and Sieg's.

It was tough for all of us to part on that third day. El had already sued me for sole custody December 1977, after I sobered up. I'd decided to not fight him about it when I found out in February '78.

My childhood had been ruptured and torn too many times for me to ever want to do that to my kids. They were fine where they were. Their dad loved them. He could afford to get them into sports and music. I didn't even have a job. They were in a stable situation. He owned the house. I always rented a two-bedroom apartment close to a good school and a playground just in case. I knew El could never survive being separated from his kids. He was not emotionally strong. I'd just survived two years without them. I didn't want to put them in the middle of a custody battle as I knew it would be brutal.

I was fortunate to have a program for living and a huge network of friends around me. I hoped that one day my kids would come to me on their own.

Looking back, I can see that leaving them under the custody of El and Nana was the worst mistake I ever made. I've regretted it my whole life. I live with the consequences every day.

I concentrated my efforts on improving myself. I did nine twelve-step series back-to-back. I needed the repetition and the support of the group. I had to get better. I went to at least one meeting a day during the first ten years in the program. I learned how to meditate, pray, and do a daily self-survey, noting the good as well as the not-so-good.

My sponsor was Carol M. We met during my first Novalco series. At the end of that eighteen-week program, I asked her to be my sponsor. I called her on the phone almost every day for seven years, to report my progress and chat about the day's happenings. Carol was truly a support for me. We had so much in common and ended up helping each other. For years, as she raised her two kids alone, she was on welfare. I remember when she got her first job in sobriety. She was so nervous that she couldn't stop throwing up. I came over early in the morning to assist her in getting ready. I had been working in an office for a few years and gave her some tips about what was expected. She was like me in that her only job experience was singing. That was all she had ever done. Some courses at night school had given her the office skills she needed. Now she just had to find the courage to go out the door.

Finally, in the nick of time, she pulled out of the driveway and went off to her first day of work. I received a phone call at lunchtime saying she was very excited. Everything was going to work out okay for my good friend.

I met a man named Don M. He seemed like a sweet person, twenty-three years my senior. Nice and safe, I thought. We started to go around to meetings together and became close friends. I watched his three boys go from being teenagers to being young men. I loved them, their partners, and their children. We had lots of family dinners, and cake and coffee for the kid's birthdays. We were there when little Nova Katrina was born and we marvelled at being Grandparents. I like the sound of being called 'Grandma Lyn'.

Carol, Gardie, Don, and I got together for dinners at my apartment. Both Carol and I were singers. After supper, the guitars came out. We loved to sing the old country standards and some of the songs I had written. She would do the harmony line.

The time I remember most fondly was when we went to see "Elvis, Elvis, Elvis" in Cloverdale. I had my picture taken with them, and one of them gave me a rose. I was in seventh heaven.

Don and I seldom missed a sobriety conference if it was held in the lower mainland of BC. We loved to dance and play games, hike, and work on jigsaw puzzles together. Every year we went to the sobriety conference in Powell River and visited with his family. They were an excellent group of people. We took a trip to Winnipeg for a relative's wedding celebration. It was a short and very cold stay. We had a really nice life for the first few years. Then we decided to get married just after my thirtieth birthday.

In 1981, I asked Carol to be my Matron of Honour. Another friend, Jose, was the Maid of Honour. My daughter, Darlene, was the flower girl, and Daniel walked me down the aisle. It was a grand ceremony. Don's brother, Bill, piped us into the hall for our reception. Groups of relatives kept going out the back door and were gone for quite a while. Then they'd come back in only to leave again a half hour later. I found out from my mom that someone had a couple bottles of booze in their truck and were hosting a tailgate party during my wedding reception, which was dry.

I don't know what I was thinking marrying him. He was twenty-three years my senior. This was a good example of my fatal flaw, 'my love will cure him'. He was not able to consummate his love for me. His alcoholism had destroyed the nerves that made it possible for him to get an erection. But, I didn't know about any of this. Since he'd studied to be a priest, I just thought he was waiting for marriage before we made love. When he couldn't be with me after marriage, I knew something was wrong. And he wasn't talking. It wasn't until my last day with him, three years later, that I understood some of what alcoholism had done to him.

The day after our wedding, Don and I drove my kids back to Salmon Arm. I took him to meet Louise and Sieg. We then toured around the Okanagan for a week before going back home and settling into married life once again.

I had some severe health issues plaguing me during my marriage to Don, but my friends were loving and supportive and that got me through it.

By the time 1984 came, I'd been seeing a doctor in New Westminster for six years as there was something wrong in my lower tummy. This pain caused me to cry out and bend over in excruciating pain. I endured her constantly making me feel like I was a crazy woman as she kept telling me that nothing was wrong.

One day, as I was getting ready to leave for work, I doubled over in pain and couldn't go on. I called my sponsor. She called the ambulance and directed them to my home. The ER doctor felt my tummy and said they were going to do emergency exploratory surgery. Good thing, too. I had a grapefruit-sized tumour on the right ovary and a baseball-sized tumour on the left, which was about to burst. They re-opened the scar from the hysterectomy in 1973 and removed my ovaries and tubes. Fortunately, the tumours were benign, and I was already on hormone replacement therapy. I was so grateful to be out of pain. It had been quite debilitating.

The following year, I had a large benign lump the size of a Christmas orange removed from my right breast. Even though it left a huge sunken area, I didn't bother having it reconstructed. My body had been through enough.

As mentioned, fatal flaw in every relationship I'd been a party to was my inability to see the person clearly. I saw the 'potential' and convinced myself that my love would cure and heal everything that was wrong and their potential would blossom and we would be happy forever. The relationship with this man was no different. There was one thing about him that drove me crazy. He talked incessantly and made himself sound like an expert on any topic. No one could get a word in edgewise, so we had no friends. I decided that if that was his worst quality, he was still better than most. I was determined to do my best.

After we married, his personality flipped. Where he had been open and flowing before, he became jealous and possessive. He accused me of wrongdoing and would not let up on me. After a few years of this, I threw in the towel and developed a plan to leave in a quiet way. I was not the confrontational type. Then he told me what he'd done to his previous wife and that scared the hell out of me. I enlisted a friend with a truck and while Don was at work the next day, I divided our possessions and food, and was about to leave him with a note of explanation.

He came home early and found me going out the door. After realizing what had happened, he chased me down the hall and out to the parking lot. He was screaming at me and, I was terrified. I just wanted to get away. I had never seen him like that and it frightened me. In one quick move, he yanked my wedding rings off my finger and turned on his heel. I drove off, crying, shaking, and relieved all at the same time. This incident made me realize that I had made the right decision. I was ready to start my new life without him. I couldn't live with the fear that he would do to me what he'd done to his ex-wife.

I was working at a company on Schoolhouse Street and had found an apartment just up the road. Don found out where I lived and tried to woo me back. Each day, as I left for work, there would be a card or a gift outside my door. One day, he left a vase of flowers. My arms were full, and I didn't see it. I heard it crunch under my foot as a piece flew up and cut my other leg. I was furious. Why wouldn't he leave me alone? I wanted a nice quiet life. There was no way I was ever going back to him. I decided I would file for divorce. To my surprise and shame, the lines had been drawn at my recovery group. People rallied around him, but few rallied around me. My sponsor was still my friend and confidante. She helped me through a really rough time in my life. Carol and my friend Louise counselled me through it.

I would still see him at the dances. It was the strangest thing to be dancing beside him on the same floor and yet not feel anything for him. There was no rage, resentment, regret or remorse. I had no feelings at all for him. I found this so hard to believe because for six years, he had meant a great deal to me. Now I just felt flat. The Spirit of the Universe had removed the burden I had been carrying. I was free to live my own life.

When I heard of his passing some years later, I didn't feel one way or the other. That made me sad. I want to go on record here and say that it takes two to tango and we both made mistakes in our relationship. I won't go into any details because his family is still living in the area and there's been enough hurt between us. Suffice to say that Don and I had a good time for four of our six years together. If I think of him at all, I will remember those years and wish him well on his Soul's journey.

I went to dances with my friends and several weeks later, I thought I'd met someone special. He seemed very present and attentive. Since my ex was not able to have an erection, it had been about seven years since I'd been with anyone.

After about six months, I consented to go to his bachelor pad for lunch. He said he was a good cook and I naively took him up on it. I had no inklings or internal warnings of any kind about his real personality.

We had a really nice lunch and sat at his chrome and yellow Formica kitchen table visiting over tea. He lowered his voice and started to woo me and gently touch my arm. I'd held off on sex because I'd been through a lot and was not really looking for more than just a good friendship – someone I could go to movies or parties with.

About fifteen minutes later, we were on the bed and getting hot and heavy. In seconds he had me cuffed to the headboard without my consent. I was instantly horrified as his demeanour had completely changed. He became menacing.

He kept me captive there for over eight hours, repeatedly raping and strangling me. I passed out several times. His sexual issue was the inability to achieve orgasm. He never lost his erection during that time, and he was huge and hurt me terribly. After he'd had enough, he drove me home as if nothing had happened. He tried to make a future date with me but I didn't commit.

He dropped me at my door. As soon as he was gone, I went to the police and filed a report. I was checked over at RCH then released after I was interviewed. They went to the address but the man was gone. He continued to stalk me for the rest of that summer but the police never caught up with him even though I called them several times.

It was one of the most terrifying times in my life. I shook for days. Emotionally, I was a wreck. I had really bad nightmares and became very cautious around men.

My throat was sore and below was, too, but no real physical damage was done. When I went to work, I wore a scarf around my neck. I looked over my shoulder for a long time. The white and orange Ford truck was easy to spot. Why the cops never caught up with him is a mystery to me.

I tried to talk to my sister about this but she cut me off and said, "Oh, is that right. Well, I hope you're done with dating weirdos now." We then went on to have our family portrait done like nothing had been said. I smiled as sweetly as ever because that was what was expected of me. That's how it is in my family.

Being a true people-pleaser, I just wanted my family to love me. So, I faked it for a while. I kept on going to family birthday cake and coffee, calling Mom every other day, and phoning my sisters. I found it very hard to carry on. Every time I thought I'd found someone special, they hurt or abused me in some way. After this last incident, I folded inward on myself. I was still going to meetings but I was covering. I went to the doctor and told him I was becoming depressed. He knew what had happened to me—again. I had samples before I even left the office. He cautioned me to take them as directed. But I didn't heed his advice. I took a few too many and ended up in the hospital.

I remember my sponsor, Carol, standing by my bed and stroking my hair. She said, "I don't think you really wanted to kill yourself, Lynnie. I think you just didn't want to hurt anymore. What's hurting you?" We talked for a few hours and I felt so much better.

I've never forgotten that and have developed good tools that will get me away from the emotional pain and mental anguish as quickly as possible.

A few months later, I was sitting at a sobriety conference, listening to a particularly good speaker. I glanced around the room to see if there was anyone I knew and could visit afterward. I almost fell off my chair when I saw D-Allan. You can imagine my surprise to see him there as I'd heard he died in a car accident a few years before. He noticed me and we struck up a conversation. We ended up going out for coffee and re-kindling the relationship that had been abandoned several years before. It wasn't surprising that I went back with someone 'safe'.

I knew he had the same defect from which my dad suffered–womanizer. That is what had broken us up the last time. I must have acquired a temporary form of insanity when I hooked up with him again.

We celebrated our renewed relationship with a trip to Long Beach. We were there for a week of sun and sand. When I got back to work on Monday, I received a call from a friend saying that my sponsor, Carol, had died of cancer. I knew she'd had a cold that wouldn't let up, but none of knew how sick she was.

Words cannot describe the pain I felt on hearing this news. It was a physical feeling in the pit of my stomach. She was a sweet person, very loving and giving. She was someone I trusted with all of my secrets. I had depended heartily upon her. When my first sponsor Gloria died of alcoholism, Carol helped me to understand more about this disease and how people could slip back into it. She and I were in a step series together. I knew that what I had found was a gift, and I didn't want to lose it. That was what drove me back to meetings, the steps, my higher power, and my sponsor. I was tired of the pain and suffering. I knew life could be really good. I had lived many of the promises noted in the Big Book. I had to get to a meeting. D-Allan was supportive of me during this time, and for that, I'll always be grateful.

A few months later, I received a call from my ex-brother-in-law, Justin, saying that El had suffered a blown aneurysm in the left side of his brain and wasn't expected to live. Justin wanted me to come up and get the kids. He said El was in the hospital in Kamloops. D-Allan and I hastily made plans.

We rented a house with three bedrooms and two bathrooms. It was close to a school in Pitt Meadows. We were so lucky that it all fell together in just a few days. We were sure that ur Higher Power was clearing a path so I could have my kids again. We wanted to provide a loving and balanced home. The time had come. I would use all of the tools I'd found in the program to help them through their grief and mourning. I would help them establish their own lives here at the coast. They could be re-introduced into my family, as their dad and nana had not allowed the kids to see them for years.

The following weekend, we went up to get the kids. We'd shared with Nana and Justin that we had the house all ready for them and had talked to the school counsellors about Daniel and Darlene's situation. We wanted to lay the groundwork for the heavy-duty grieving we were sure would ensue. They said they would get the kids ready to bring down.

When we arrived, we were met with a cold reception and a big fat "No" as to our suitability to parent these children—my children. We had been told that we could have custody, and that is why we had made all of the arrangements. We were so disappointed. I tried to reassure the kids, but I didn't know what would happen to them.

Nana was quite senior in years and none of El's siblings were able or willing to take them in. Seeing how close Daniel and Darlene were and how clung to each other in their fear and grief, Nana called Social Services and told them that the kids were sexual with each other, and it would be best if they were separated.

Social Services stepped in, and the kids were put in foster homes at either end of Salmon Arm. A once close relationship with each other was rent by the system. It was déjà vu for me. I hated the fact that I was separated from my children, and they were distanced from each other.

The year after I came into the program, I went to PVI Business College and acquired some office skills. However, in my first year of sobriety, I'd moved eight times and did various odd jobs just to survive. I wanted more than that for my kids, and now they were going to be living in a foster home, just like I had. It was very hard to take.

In retrospect, I can see a special design in the details of my life. Only a few days before we received the call about El, I had been laid off from my job at a battery company. This left me free to find the house, talk to the school, query my friends on rules for raising teens, and go up to Salmon Arm. But it was not meant to be, at this time.

I was very good at Credit and Collections and had a solid work record. I had gone on some interviews that should have gone my way but they didn't. I couldn't understand why. I had to get a job so I could get my kids.

Convinced that he was the reason my in-laws had said "No", I separated from D-Allan and my sister Sasha kindly took me in until I could get on my feet.

She was a witness to my struggle and a loving support for me. I got a lawyer, went to Family Court and fought almost daily for a year. The woman at Salmon Arm Social Services kept telling me that I needed to become my kids' Foster Parent. I had to jump through all of their hoops before they would let me have custody. I had to prove myself as a fit parent. She said I would receive a benefit and I would then be able to support them. Since I didn't have a job, I thought this was the only way I would be able to do it. I was submitted to a battery of tests by all kinds of professionals and had a police check done.

Eight months later, I sat in the office of this social worker as she smirked at me. "You are not getting one red cent out of this department", she said, as she chewed on the centre of her pencil.

I told her "I never wanted your money anyway. I only want my children. This was all your idea and I'm so happy this department is satisfied with my ability to look after my own kids." I was going to keep my cool at all costs to my pride. My mom had been on welfare and I could be too, temporarily, if need be. The important thing was getting my kids into a stable home—my home.

I'd used the last of my UI to put a deposit on a three-bedroom apartment for the three of us. I didn't know what we were going to do but I was sure that with a family and support group like mine, we would not be going hungry.

I left her office being ever-so-glad to be rid of her and Salmon Arm Social Services. I had my kids, and I was thrilled. A friend of mine had volunteered himself and his truck so we went to pick up Daniel and his belongings. Darlene would not be coming down for another month.

It was tough slugging. I never knew where the next meal was coming from. I visited the food bank regularly. Friends brought over fresh fruit and vegetables. I accepted charity with mixed feelings of guilt and gratitude. We made it day-by-day. But you know, there wasn't one day that I went without a cigarette. When I look back at this now, I'm amazed at my audacity to still smoke under these circumstances. I was hooked on nicotine; a slave to yet another vice.

According to the Universe, I had the cart before the horse because on the fourth of September, after Darlene had come down and we were settled in our apartment, I got a job. The ad was written just for me. The income was sufficient and they offered extended benefits plus paid vacation.

On October 31, 1987, sole and permanent custody was granted to me from the Province of British Columbia. Estranged no more, we were a family. It was a day to celebrate, and we did.

FEAR – "FEELING EDGY AND RETICENT"

I was saying to Louise the other day that I'm not really afraid of dying. I am afraid of fear.

I am allergic to bees and wasps so I carry an EPI pen. If a wasp just flies by and stings me, I will use my EPI pen to save my life. If a wasp flies by and starts to harass me by flying in my face and bombing my head, then I become afraid that I will be stung. And that is what I fear… being afraid. Why? Because I become irrational and have actually run out into street traffic, and almost fallen down a flight of stairs to get away from a wasp.

If someone breaks into my house and murders me in my sleep, then I'm dead. But if someone breaks into my house and tortures me, then I am afraid. And that is what I fear… that kind of mental 'going off the track' and 'out of my mind'.

So, what I fear most is going out of my mind and not being myself enough to keep myself safe.

In February 1984, I was so afraid that I could no longer leave my house, and I became agoraphobic. I was trapped for almost six months before I found help from a man named Jim at Se-Cure in Vancouver. He taught me how to face these fears. I started by listing them all. I include the list here because you won't believe it, if I don't. This list is in the original order that these fears came to me as I wrote:

Fire, water, bees, wasps, the dark, death, ridicule, rejection, strangers, talking to a large group of people, performing in front of a small group, enclosed spaces, open spaces, driving (especially on bridges), escalators, elevators, being in an accident, seeing an accident, messiness, being raped, offending people, strong emotional behaviour being expressed in my presence, failure, becoming angry myself, really trying hard, dentists, germs/bacteria, being ill, cancer, blood/bleeding, losing my singing voice, losing my vision, losing my hearing, letting go, being helpless, my kids dying, being sexually undesirable, being sexually desirable, my sexual fantasies, disorder, being attacked and tortured, tall handsome men, my husband dying, being out of control, being vulnerable, choking, the occult, being murdered, never making it, having an orgasm when someone else is there, evil, the devil, UFO's, spirits, venereal disease, aggressiveness in me, aggressiveness in others, my rage, losing my mind, psych ward, being fired, ruining something important at work, going crazy and no one can put me back together again, never getting another job, being like my Mother, losing my Mother, not being like my Mother, being a 'runner' like my Father, and competition.

These seventy-one fears got so out of hand that they bound me up tight. One time, when I went to the dentist to get a filling, I was so full of fear that I bolted right out of the chair and ran blindly out into a vicious snowstorm. I left my shoes and coat at the office. My solution—I would 'save up' the dental work and a hundred bucks and then get it all done at the same time under a general anesthetic.

After going through the Se-Cure program, I went off coffee for a year as it causes anxiety in some people. At that point, I was drinking up to twenty cups a day. A few years before, I'd switched from booze and pills to coffee when I joined a twelve-step program on October

22, 1977. It seems that even coffee will have its way with me, if I overuse it.

I've always had some unreasonable fears and I still do. This was an acute situation and as I weaned myself off coffee and stuck to the daily rigors of the program Jim outlined, I started to come out of this dark place and emerge once more into the light.

I renewed my knowledge of meditation and deep breathing so that I could come back to a centred place within myself. It has been a long and arduous journey of self-discovery. I have met my dark side and it is me. I'm not afraid anymore. I have a daily reprieve contingent on my spiritual condition.

Today, (February 2002) I had a root canal and experienced no fear and no pain. The power of meditation and an excellent dentist is a marriage made in heaven. I say my prayers, do some deep breathing, and float up into a big bubble above the dentist. From there, I can watch the procedure and feel very relaxed and serene. I have complete confidence in my dentist, and his very competent staff. They always make me feel safe, secure, and important.

In the past, I have had dentists who worked on three or four patients at the same time. They would flit from one chair to another never paying any attention to ME. They would discuss things with each other and sometimes these topics were private. I didn't want to know this stuff and yet they continued to talk over me as if I were not even there. This sort of dentist has a business, the sole purpose of which is to make money and allow himself and his staff to have a 'really fun day', as I was told so often by them.

I feel quite different with my new dentist. His care and concern have all but wiped out the previous tortures I have experienced in the dreaded dentist's chair. His complete attention is focused on my well-being. He stays with me from beginning to end. He even cleans my teeth. When he administers the freezing, he massages my gums and jaw and does not do anything until I am well frozen. I know about his family and he knows about mine. We talk to each other as people. We work together to make sure I am getting the finest dental treatment that I can.

He is the true tooth fairy. It is he who is enabling me to keep my teeth as long as I can. I tell him often that I appreciate his dental artistry and why this means so much to me. I would recommend him to anyone especially those filled with fear, as I was when I went to see him three years ago.

One fear down, seventy to go. Progress not perfection.

A HOUSE OF CARDS

It had been a tough couple of years since D-Allan and I had gone our separate ways. I'd had a few relationships and it had always ended the same way. I would get a call and they would say, "I've met the girl of my dreams and it is not you, so bye-bye now." The details don't matter anymore. I was becoming disillusioned with the dating scene. It never was my thing, anyway. I was the marrying kind and really disliked all of the fooforah that went on beforehand. It seemed so false.

I'd been seeing 'John' for six months. We'd talked on the phone that morning at ten. He asked if I could please drive this time so he could drink. I said I would pick him up at 8:30 p.m. as we'd decided to go to the dance. At 3:30, he called me back to say he had met the girl of his dreams the night before and he couldn't see me again. (Huh? *We* were together the night before.)

A few months before, I had gone for counselling and had done a 'man plan' with Bev, the counsellor. This required I write down the qualities I would like in a partner and think about them every day.

I knew John was not the man for me. Still, I was stunned. He was fun and we had a good time. What is that old saying about 'don't let the good be the enemy of the best'?

I started to cry. My daughter wasn't having any of it. She hadn't thought much of John to begin with. She now went about getting me ready for the evening. At the appropriate time, she booted me out the door and told me to have a good time. My sister, Catharine, had just had back surgery so I visited her in the hospital then went on to the dance.

I met some of my girlfriends and sat with them. John showed up with the 'girl of his dreams' and I felt sick. When I saw her going into the bathroom, I followed her in there. I was going to tell her what a jerk he was and what he had done to me earlier in the day. I wanted to warn her off him. I decided against that tactic because I don't know what God's will was for her (or for him either). I let it go and went back to my table.

The band was terrible but I still got out on the dance floor for almost every song. I loved to move my body in time to the beat. I closed my eyes and allowed myself to be swept away and healed by the music. Each note penetrated my psyche and smoothed out the bumps of the day.

They were playing a Paul Jones (the one where you have to go and get another partner each time they say the words 'Paul Jones'). I saw three guys lined up by the bar. They were definitely 'my type': dark wavy hair, doe-brown eyes, and big husky guys. I started to head towards them when I thought, *Hey, haven't you had enough!* I veered to the right and saw a man sitting beside the coffee pot. He had his legs crossed and was surveying the crowd. I made a beeline for him and asked him to join me.

He said, "Yes", and we began to move around the floor. After a few fast ones, a slow song was played.

Holding out his arms, he said, "Shall we?"

I said, "Sure."

As I slipped into his arms, an electric shock coursed through me from the top of my head, down my spine, and into Mother Earth. I felt grounded, connected, and alive.

We glided around the hall and made small talk.

He said, "So, how long have you been on your own?"

I looked at my watch and answered, "Oh, about six hours."

We laughed and started to talk about our kids. My two were preppies and his was a head-banger. We went back to our respective tables after he secured a promise of more dances later in the evening.

The girls wanted to know all about him, so I told them what I had found out so far. He worked at a chemical plant in Port Moody and had just been hired on full time after being on contract for a year. He was in his late forties and had separated from his wife two years previous. His younger daughter had just moved in with him not long before. His older daughter lived close by. He wasn't going to come tonight as he had been studying his first aid homework and was tired. But he decided that since it was Saturday night, he should make the effort to have some fun. They were impressed that I had learned so much in such a short time. *They* didn't know what *I* did… I had finally found 'the one'. I just knew it!

I turned down a couple of other guys hoping he would come over and we could dance some more. I had my back to the dance floor as I talked with one of my friends. I turned when I heard my name. Norm was standing at the end of the table, drink in hand, asking if he could join us. Now it was my turn to say "Yes".

We didn't sit down until the next break. At the end of the evening, he asked if he could walk me to my car. We headed out the door and through the parking lot. Having reached my little Chevy, I took out my keys. He looked at my car and said, "Wow, I have a car just like yours, except mine has four wheels." What he meant to say was four doors. But that wouldn't have been near as funny as the comment he did make. We laughed and it felt good, considering the day I'd had. He said he would call me in a few days. I really hoped he would.

On Sunday, the kids and I did the laundry and shopping, and got things ready for school and work on Monday.

Norm didn't call, and I hoped I hadn't done something to put him off. I wanted to get to know him better. I decided I was not going to call him as I had done this in the past, and it never worked out. As enlightened as we all like to think we are, there are some things that are hard to change. It was still up to the man to show interest and make the overtures.

It was month-end at work, and I was very busy the next day but not so busy that I didn't have time to check him out. I had two kids that I loved with all of my heart. They depended on me to keep them safe. I wasn't about to let some weirdo into their lives. I had been fooled many times before.

This time, I needed to be extra careful. I called around and talked to a few people. I did everything within my power and scope up to but not including a financial credit check. That would have been an invasion of privacy that was uncalled for. I just wanted to make sure that he didn't have a criminal record. I didn't care what kind of money he made.

He checked out okay and I felt more comfortable. I couldn't wait for him to call that night. After all, it had been a 'few days'. No call came.

Nothing unusual happened the next day, and still no call from Norman.

On the Wednesday night I was watching TV with the phone on my lap. When the phone rang, I jumped and it went crashing to the floor. I was trying not to sound like a giggly schoolgirl even though that's how I felt. He said he would like to take me out to the dance on Saturday night. I asked him if we really had to wait for Saturday, couldn't we have drinks or something the night before. He agreed. I was delighted.

We went for a walk on Crescent Beach and then out for coffee on the Friday night. It was a delightful October night–cool and clear, with stars and that midnight blue sky. We talked and walked the length on the beach. He was funny and we laughed a lot.

Born in Northolt (a borough of Ealing; in the county of Middlesex), a suburb of London, England, he had the loveliest of accents so it was very relaxing to listen to him. He told captivating stories about events in his life. He shared about his daughters and what they were doing. He talked about his career in drafting and design and about his current position as a maintenance supervisor in a chemical plant.

I found him very attractive. He moved with grace and dignity, and he was extremely easy to look at: finely chiseled features, grey/green eyes, and brown hair. He seemed to be taken with me, too.

We ended the evening with a promise of seeing each other the next night.

The next few months are a blur of dining, dancing, movies, family outings, getting to know each other's children, and introducing him to my huge family. I found out that his family, which included his two girls, and his Dad, who lived in Victoria, was a little smaller than my family of twenty-three people (siblings, husbands, and children). He also mentioned he had a cousin, Wayne and his wife, Judy, who lived in Dartmouth, Nova Scotia.

In December, we decided to merge his family and mine under one roof. We all went looking for a home large enough to accommodate

Norm and I, and our three kids, all nine months apart at ages fourteen, fifteen and sixteen. We knew it was going to be a challenge as Norm and I had known each other only three and a half months and we had both just got custody of our teen kids. Also, we had both just started work in our new business positions. We took a giant leap of faith that what we had would be enough to hold us together during the tough times ahead.

Over the next year, we had a lot of adjusting to do. We added a couple of cats, some birds, and an aquarium to our family. I read books about blended families and talked to some of my friends who were in the same position.

Since they were all at an age where they wanted to get their driver's licence and I was the parent with the most patience, I was elected to teach them. I taught Daniel and Janice how to drive. It was a pleasure to see them go from being a non-driver to a good driver. We started out in the school parking lot and graduated to Highway 99. This was one of the best experiences for me as a Mother at the time. I often look back and cherish that special time spent with the kids.

Darlene was another story. While we were in the school parking lot going over the basics, I asked her to put her right foot on the brake. She used her left foot. I told her she needed to use her right foot and she insisted she was doing so. At that moment, I knew it would take someone more skilled than I to teach my dear daughter to drive. 'Young Drivers of Canada' came to the rescue. All of our kids are conscientious drivers, today. I trust them with my life and the lives of our grandchildren.

Each of us was so different and from such varied backgrounds. You'd have hardly thought that any of us were related at all. But I was sure that our love would conquer and win the battle of wits fought out each day in our home.

Norm and I would sometimes escape to our bedroom, and it became a safe haven where we could converse in quiet and forget about the petty bickering that would ensue around issues of chores and belongings. They were, after all, old enough to sort these things out in an orderly fashion. Well, as you can see by my attitude, I was quite naïve. All the reading and talking had not prepared me in the least. I was at a loss as to know how to make it work, though I wanted to with all of my heart.

I was still in my 'Norman Rockwell' phase. This hurt our chances of ever becoming a solid family. We were fragmented and living like strangers. I tried to tell myself happy little stories about our strained lives, but that's all they were—stories. There was nothing romantic or real about it. What was real was the fact that my kids were hurting terribly about what had happened to their father. Norm's daughter was acting out because her parents had split up. And, truthfully, Norm and I didn't know each other, at all. Why we thought we could ever put it together so quickly, even though our intentions were good, is beyond me. We'd been blinded by love.

His daughter was the first to go. There were words exchanged about some trivial thing like what time she had to be home, or whom she was hanging out with, and she took off with her friends and ended up living on the streets of Vancouver for eleven days. We didn't know where she was or how to get in touch with her. One thing led to another, and she ended up going to stay with her sister and then with her mother. We had limited contact with her. The relationship was strained for several years to come.

My son was next to go. There was real concern about his choice of friends and the honesty in those relationships. I asked him to reconsider his situation as we felt it was quite serious. This didn't fly. He became rude and withdrew from us. We didn't know what was in his heart and mind and he wasn't talking.

We decided to get a family counsellor in to sort us all out. Still, he would not talk to us. He would go on about how his friends understood him and what a cool guy his girlfriend's dad was. In anger one day I asked him, "If you love your friends so much, why don't you just go live with them so we could have a little peace around the house?" He moved out, leaving behind a nasty letter that was to wound me for years to come. We didn't speak for four years and four months. His choice, not mine.

Sometimes, while I was going to work, I would see my son waiting for the bus. I wanted to stop and talk with him but I was afraid I would drive him further away. I called him on his birthday and at Christmas just to let him know that I loved him and would let bygones be bygones should he ever want to resume our relationship. Then, out of the blue, he called me and came over for lunch. I don't know why he left, and I don't know why he came back. These things have never been discussed between us and I doubt they ever will. This made our relationship very fragile. I felt like I was walking on eggshells with him for years to come.

These were hurtful times for all of us. We all did and said things that we regretted later. My daughter was left in the middle, holding the bag for everyone. She became 'the good child'. Outwardly, she seemed to be doing everything right, and we touted her around and showed her off as our success. Years later, we found out about all the stuff she'd done on the sly (as most teenagers do). But what was she to do? She was accustomed to being a parental caretaker, having lived with her father for nine years, absorbing parts of his and Nana's personas, as well as being the peacemaker between her dad and her brother, Daniel.

We had been overly optimistic about our abilities to build a healthy family unit from such wounded children. We were wounded ourselves. We had no basis in reality to support the structure, and we didn't have the skills necessary to effect lasting changes. I suppose all parents just do the best they can. I wish we had done a whole lot better.

If I had had my way, when the kids were on their own, I would have had them over for Sunday supper at least once a month. I remember all the fun times I had at various family dinners. I know that this can forge relationships and keep them current. I would like to have had the opportunity to create that for our kids. Unfortunately, their schedules don't permit this due to shift work, and Norm's daughter lives on the island. Today, we are phone buddies. This is a very good thing.

The relationship with my father was the wild card upon which my house of cards was built. Because of that, all of my future relationships were tainted. Until I decided to let him go with love, there was little chance of forming a trusting bond with anyone else.

I have stopped trying to get in touch with my father. While viewing an *Oprah* program in June 1996, I made a break-through regarding my father. I'd mailed him a huge package of material all about me. It included copies of achievement awards, certificates, career reviews, poems, prose, short stories, songs I had written, and photos of my husband, kids, and grandkids. I made him a Father's Day card and sent it off in the mail in an effort to tell him who I had become and how I was doing. I was hoping he would be proud of me and that he would want to get to know me. I was wrong.

I didn't hear a word for three months. At the end of August, I received a letter from his son, Michael Hugo MacKay. My heart stopped when I read the return address. I thought he was writing to say that our dad had died. I stood in front of my mailbox and read the letter like a starving person eats a piece of mouldy bread. Three quarters of the way through, he said, "By the way, Dad says 'hi'". I was furious. After three months of checking the mail, wondering, waiting, having fantasies about my dad making his way to me at last, having the horrors about my dad being dead and it being too late for us, being angry and ashamed that he didn't love me because I wasn't good enough, what do I get? "By the way, Dad says 'hi'", indeed.

That was a defining moment for me. It spoke volumes and I it heard for the first time. He didn't care. He never did. It didn't have anything to do with me as a person. It had everything to do with the fact that he was just a screwed-up guy who had no idea what he was missing by not getting to know my family and me, along with his other five kids, and eight Grandkids, and three Great-Grandkids and all of their families. His sister, Bessie, is alive and well and would probably love to see him after she got through smacking him upside of the head.

I had brought a lot of baggage into my relationship with Norm. It was frustrating and challenging, but we were sorting through it a day at a time. Norm had quite a temper, in those days. Every once in a while, it caught up with him, and he would explode all over the place. At those times, I wondered if we would ever make it. I didn't do well in a topsy-turvy world. I needed stability. I needed a safe haven from the world in which I was forced to operate. I needed a place to call home.

TO HAVE AND TO HOLD

S everal months before the rift in our relationship with my son, Norm asked me to marry him. Norm, Daniel, and Darlene had planned the surprise. He donned his tuxedo and waited for his unsuspecting partner to walk through the door. I was escorted up to the living room and asked to take a seat on the couch. Then Norm came in and knelt before me with single red rose between his teeth. He told me how much he loved me and what it meant to him to have me in his life. Tears glistened in his eyes. I laughed, cried, and said "yes" when he popped the question.

We set the date for a few months later. One night, as we ate our meal at the Bonanza Restaurant, we planned our Wedding Day. Using several napkins, we mapped out the details: who to invite, what to say on the invitations, what to wear, who would be in the bridal party, the feast, the music, the first dance, and all of the myriad details that go into planning a wedding day.

We had become close friends with my sister, Victoria, and her partner, Thomas. They were to be our Matron of Honour and Best Man. Our song is "Always" by Atlantic Starr. We asked our kids to sing it for us after we said our vows. We wrote words of love and devotion to say to each other to say in front of our family and friends.

Fifty people were invited and we ended up seating forty-two in our living room. We placed candles and fresh flowers on every surface to create a romantic ambiance. Rather than go with a particular colour scheme, we went with several–pastel shades of blue, pink, yellow, green and purple. A sumptuous buffet covered the top of our covered pool table in the den.

We were sequestered in our room and watched through the window as our guests arrived. Alternately pensive and excited, the anticipation mounted. Finally, we heard the music swell and our escorts were at the bedroom door. We walked down the hall and turned to the left. Just as we came into the dining room, Norm's knees buckled, and we both thought he would fall over. He took a deep breath, found his feet, and we gracefully made our entrance with no one the wiser.

The ceremony proceeded smoothly until it was time to say our vows. All of a sudden, a plane flew over the house, and this set mom's dog, Taffy, to yapping. She barked all the way through our promises to each other. But, I heard Norm, and he heard me. That's all that matters, in the end. It was a light-filled sunny day. We had found a love to last. Surrounded by our family and friends, what more could anyone ask. I said a silent prayer of thanks. On May 20, 1989, at 11:17 a.m., we were pronounced husband and wife. One of the best days of my life.

The reception was held downstairs. We had a dance floor and lots of room for everyone to party on. At five o'clock, we made our get-away.

We'd planned a weekend to Harrison Hot Springs for our honeymoon. After a delicious dinner at the Hot Springs Hotel, we had a little nap thinking we'd take a walk on the beach and enjoy the moonlight before retiring for the night. We woke up ten hours later at 6:00 a.m. the next morning. So much for our wedding night.

"Well, that's okay," we told each other. "There's always today and the rest of our lives."

I was craving coffee so my new husband set out to find me a 'cuppa'. Upon his return, he told me this story... First, he tried the front desk. They were brewing a pot but it was for the staff only. He got in the car and started searching around Harrison but to no avail. He went as far as Agassiz but still no luck. He drove back to the hotel and spotted a man carrying the black brew. The man said there was a little coffee shop up a side street so Norm jumped back in the car and tore off up the street. He bought us each two cups of coffee and hastily made his way back to our room.

I'd started to get worried as he'd been gone for over half an hour. I'd had a shower and gotten ready for a day of exploring. I so appreciated his efforts in getting me a cup of coffee to start my day. I drink two cups in the morning to kick-start the old bod and I really miss it if I don't get it.

We went into the restaurant for breakfast and then off to see the sites of the town.

After lunch, we were moved to go back to our room and pick up where we had left off the night before. I guess it wasn't meant to be as just when things were getting heated up, someone knocked at the door. We both made a dash for cover because it startled us. It was room service with a complimentary bottle of champagne and a certificate of congratulations. After the shock wore off, we relaxed back into what we'd been doing. Our love-making was always somewhat spectacular and we practised as often as we could, to get it just right.

We hung out with my sister, Victoria and her partner, Thomas. We all had teenagers at home so when we would get together, the old soapbox would come out and circulate around the room. It was a safe way to be able to vent openly and get some support from people who were going through similar things to us.

Thomas and Norman were like brothers, each from the UK, and very close. They had both grown up in Great Britain and had some interesting 'sayings' that always got Victoria and I to raising our eyebrows and chuckling to ourselves.

One day, we decided to take 'the boys' to Victoria for Father's Day. Not telling them where we were going, we left the house at six in the morning. Victoria had dug up some blinds for them to wear so they couldn't see. We drove to Surrey and had breakfast. Then we pulled out the masks and had Norm put on the elephant one and Thomas, the doggie one. I took a circuitous route to the ferry and they were trying to guess which way we were going. It was hilarious.

As we approached the terminal, Victoria got out of the car and walked up to the booth to explain the spectacle about to arrive, ask for silence, and purchase our passage. The looks we got as we drove past the attendants were priceless. They were laughing hysterically and doing their best to keep quiet, pointing and gesticulating. I guess they'd seen everything now. It wasn't until I drove over the ramp that the guys surmised we were going on the ferry.

Arriving in Sidney, we drove on to Victoria. Our goal was to have high tea at the Empress Hotel. There was time to explore so we walked around the town and ended up at Beacon Park. We fooled around like teenagers, chasing each other around trees, and tumbling on the grass. We had a wondrous and free time for a while.

Then we went back to the hotel to change. I discovered to my dismay that, in the dark that morning, I had grabbed one black high heel and one black flat. I ended up wearing my sandals. We didn't know we needed a reservation, so our hopes for high tea were dashed. But all was not lost. We headed downstairs and had 'low tea' and a fantastic dessert that looked more like a piece of art.

We went to Victoria again for my fortieth. We had adjoining house-keeping rooms with a little kitchen. On the day of my birthday, the radio was playing and Victoria and I were dancing in the kitchen. We were laughing and thoroughly enjoying ourselves. The guys were loading up the car.

All of a sudden, I was on the floor and unable to breath. From far away, I could hear Victoria yelling "Lynnie, Lynnie!" I had never thought that I would make it to forty, considering the kind of life I'd led with the booze and the drugs and the guys, some of whom had tried to kill me. Many times my life had been on the line. Now, it seemed to be decision time. Was I going to stay or go? I chose to stay. I was in a sparkling blue area with high-pitched sounds. It was a crystal clear decision, and I have never regretted it.

My consciousness returned to the room, and Victoria helped me to my feet. Only minutes had passed but it had seemed like hours. Temporarily subdued, we continued on with our day, driving up the island to play mini-golf in Parksville.

Norm and I had discovered Newport the year before while we were on our way to California Redwood Forest. We had stayed for a couple of days and explored the waterfront and a few of the beaches. Then it was time to continue on our holiday. As we were crossing over the Yaquina Bay Bridge, I felt like crying. I asked Norm why we had to go on. We had both fallen in love with the city, and there was a lot to see and do. We agreed there was no need to go any further.

We headed back over the bridge and booked into the motel we'd left only an hour before. Our vacation was relaxing and exciting. I was enthusiastic about the Oregon Coast.

We wanted to share the wonders of Newport with our dear friends, Victoria and Thomas, so a few months later, the four of us drove down.

We stayed once more at the Penny Saver where, in the morning, they offer fresh fruit, pastries, and coffee.

Thomas and I tried to play badminton on Nye Beach but the wind was fierce that day. Victoria and I enjoyed shopping for souvenirs and presents for our kids at the many little gift marts along the way. We walked through the bay front and saw the Stellar Sea Lions on the wharf. There were so many, that it almost tipped over. Their continuous honking offered an appropriate background to the smell of the sea, the cries of the gulls and the taste of salt-water taffy.

We went for tea and dessert at the Apple Peddler. Later, we had supper at the Galley Ho, introducing them to all of our favourite haunts.

We headed up the Coast Highway on 4th of July, cutting over at Lincoln City and joining the I-5 at Portland. Along the way, we saw fireworks in celebration of Independence Day. As the day dimmed to dusk, we crossed the border into Canada and drove the rest of the way home in quiet reverie.

We always enjoyed the time we spent with this companionable couple, my sister and her husband. There was never any tension between them. This is how Norm and I are, as well. We don't have a lot of conflict. We all loved to sing to the Traveling Wilbury's and Garth Brooks. There was laughter and joy. It was a fun break whenever we got together with Victoria and Thomas.

By 2002, Norm and I had enjoyed the Oregon Coast fourteen times. Seven were spent at the Surf and Sand Motel, which was situated on a golden bluff above the beach. We had a one hundred and eighty degree view so we could see north up to Beverly Beach and south to the Yaquina Bay Lighthouse.

We explored that strip of sand dozens of times, always discovering something new and appreciating what we had already seen. The erosion was visible each time we visited. The storms that pound the Oregon Coast pummel stone, shells, and sea glass into sand. All that remains is the hard black basalt sculptures—shiny monoliths. Long kelp strands and old dead driftwood are heaped up and tossed high on the shore, looking like a headdress Medusa would wear.

We witnessed one of those horrendous storms as we sat in our cozy housekeeping room high above the booming foam. The funniest thing we remember is the sea gulls trying to fly against the wind and staying in one spot in mid-air; posing, as it were, for photos and sketches.

I was inspired to write some of my best poems and prose while we were in Newport. These are included in my book called "Of This Space and Time", a collection of poems, prose, and haiku.

As we were out and about, we noticed that around eighty percent of RVers had a pet in tow, usually a small dog. This got me to thinking… and Norm says that's always a scary idea—me thinking. Anyway, the yearning for a pet got really bad in 1995. Finally, we decided to get a little doggie for a companion. We started by putting our name out to the local pounds and shelters but they only had larger dogs and our complex forbids anything over a certain size. We combed pet stores and newspaper ads for several months. Finally, just after Christmas, I saw an ad for a 'miniature black poodle, four months old, housebroken, first shots'. I called the number and spoke with the fellow for half an hour.

We had never thought of having a Poodle (too hoity-toity for us). We'd been thinking more along the lines of a Beagle, Shih Tzu, Lhasa Apso, or Dachshund.

I spoke with Norm and we decided to go ahead. The owner of this dog was willing to drive down from Kamloops that afternoon. My husband and I went out for lunch and tossed around some names for our new pooch. We tried them out on our server at Wendy's to get her opinion. He already had the name 'Pikies Black Dannyboy' on his Canadian Kennel Club papers. We came up with 'Muttly'. Our new dog had a pedigree and we didn't want him to get a swelled head about it. We thought the name, 'Muttly', would keep him right-sized and humble.

When the truck pulled up in our driveway and the man got out holding a little black ball of fuzz, I thought my heart would drown in joy. He put the little thing on the pathway, and it struggled up the stairs and into my waiting arms. I fell in love. Now, six years later, he takes a flying leap off the top stair and lands about half way along the path into the yard.

His spirit is joyous, playful, and free. His love for us is unlimited. How we ever lived without him is beyond me. He has helped me through some very tough times. I will always appreciate it.

It was a challenge to incorporate him into our lives. Old habits like sleeping through the night, stepping into un-chewed shoes, and walking on a 'dry' floor, die hard. He was not housebroken. But he had a sweet demeanour and has become a true companion and friend to us. He is a part of our family.

Norm and I enjoy whale watching. Our first trip out was up in Telegraph Cove in September 1990. Stubb Island Charters ran the tour and we had booked on for the afternoon shift. When we reached deeper waters, white-sided dolphins ran the bow waves as we plowed through the sea. We were headed to Johnstone Straight, and, in particular, to Robson Bight and the rubbing beaches. We met up with A-pod, a lively group of resident Orcas, and kept them company for six hours. The crew served dinner and a beverage. It was an experience worth repeating, so we went out with them again in September 1992.

We have gone on three other whale watching trips. Once out of Ucluelet to see the grey whales; then out of Bellingham where we saw several minke whales, transient killer whales, grey whales, pilot whales, and several bottle-nosed dolphins; and finally, we went out while in Newport and saw more grey whales.

It is something that never ceases to inspire awe within my spirit. The size of these mammals, the scope of the ocean, the smallness of the people we are with and the boat we are on, conspire to make me feel humble and grateful for the opportunity to witness nature up close and personal.

Norm is a draftsman and machinist by trade. One day, as I was watching him print something, it struck me that he was an artist. It was such a strong impression that, since then, I have never looked at him any other way. For his birthday that year, I bought him a beginner's watercolour kit. He couldn't fathom why I would do such a thing, as he had never tried anything creative to that point. I knew he could paint and encouraged him. Lucky for me, I was right. From then on, we decided to only have original artwork, by ourselves or people we knew, on our walls.

Sometimes he was bored and took out his paint box. The next thing we knew, Norm was doing watercolours, charming ones. It has brought joy and serenity to us ever since.

When we next visited Sieg and Louise to celebrate our joint anniversaries, he took along his paintings to show them. They were a real hit, garnering much praise and adulation. In conversation, I commented, "I could never do what Norm has done. I can't even draw a stickman."

Louise said, "Of course you can, dear child. It's just a matter of following a few simple rules. Basically-trees are triangle shaped with the point at the top; as things go away from you, they get smaller and lighter; decide where the sun or light is coming from and put the shadow on the other side; keep things simple, less is more; just give the illusion, a touch, and so on.

When I got home, I decided to try out her concepts. I took a piece of scrap paper that was on the table and drew a simple scene of a stream, tree, mountain, lake, meadow, and an old fence fading off in the distance. When Norm came home from work, he was impressed with my efforts.

I am impatient by nature. So when I was choosing which medium I was going to take up, I decided on acrylic paints as they dry quickly. I have been painting ever since. The lesson for me is, I never know what is in me until I make an effort to ferret it out.

During the spring of 1999, I went with my daughter and son-in-law to pre-natal classes and became part of the birthing team for my first grandchild. On May 14th at mid-night, my son-in-law called to say Darlene was in labour. We drove over the bridge to pick them up and back over the bridge to the hospital. It was the ever-popular Braxton-Hicks trick, commonly called false labour. Delivering them back across the bridge at dawn, we had breakfast then came home and wearily climbed into bed.

Sleeping until noon was unheard of in our house. We are usually 'up with the rooster'. However, on this day, we stayed in bed until eleven. Burt called again and once more, we crossed the bridge to pick them up. It seemed like the real thing this time.

My daughter amazed us all with her composure, focus, and dedication to a drug-free delivery. I was so proud of her. It was very difficult to see her in the throes of labour and childbirth. I was happy that Norm and I could be there to support both of them through this wondrous experience.

Things were progressing along but I really thought we would be there until mid-night as this was her first delivery.

At 5:45 p.m., she said she wanted to push. We called the doctor in and found out that Darlene was fully dilated. We began in earnest to coach her through the final stages of breathing.

My husband, Norm, had backed off into the shadows, not knowing what to do next. The doctor asked me to assist with something, but I didn't have the physical stamina, so Norm was called into action.

I moved to the other side of the table and stood in front of my son, Daniel. Burt and Norm were across from each other. The baby was coming. I moved to the foot of the table and stood beside the doctor. Daniel was right behind me. Together, we all witnessed the birth of Connie. It was a miracle. It was such a distinct feeling, the shift in the energy—first I didn't feel her there then I did. A new person was born into the world.

I became aware that three nurses were standing in the shadows. I had not noticed them before. I took some photos as Burt held his daughter and cried. I turned into Daniel's arms and wept with joy. The doctor's eyes were glistening and Norm was tearing up, too. I took some shots of Darlene with her new little girl and then asked the doctor to take a picture of the birthing team—Daniel, Burt, Darlene, me, and Norm.

My tiny granddaughter was placed on a little shelf with heat lamps shining on her. She opened her eyes and looked right at me. We connected and have been joined at the hip ever since. She is my heart.

Connie Marie Aspen was born on 15 May at the Royal Columbian Hospital in New Westminster. This is the same hospital in which I had been born forty-seven years earlier.

'Connie' is a new name in the family. 'Marie' was the name of her dad's grandma (her great-grandma). Darlene liked the name 'Aspen'.

Spiritually, it means 'whispering tree' and it is sacred to the Celts. It symbolizes determination in overcoming fears and doubts. My first granddaughter has had to do a lot of that as her parents were always fighting, even after they divorced and that completely affected her.

I took a few days off work and visited with Darlene in the hospital. Burt's mom and Nana Marie came down from Kamloops and stayed with them at the apartment for a few days.

Then came the arduous task of teaching the little one how to suckle. My daughter was persistent and patient beyond belief. These things, I remember. My daughter was a good mother to baby Connie.

When I went back to work a few days later, I felt like I was driving the wrong way, heading west towards the office instead of east towards my daughter, son-in-law, and new granddaughter. Over time, things got back to normal. Each time I see Connie, I am awed that she is here, my granddaughter.

Norm and I are both photographers, and sometimes our equipment bag gets a little unmanageable. But when you reach the scene, if you don't have the lenses required what is the point. We found this to be the case when we took a trip to Dartmouth, Nova Scotia to visit with Norm's cousin Wayne and his wonderful wife, Judy. Our equipment bag seemed to take on a life of its own. We used everything we brought with us, though, and got all the shots we wanted to commemorate the holiday.

The scenery was breathtaking but the best part was meeting Wayne and Judy. Wayne is hilarious and bigger than life. Judy is a kind person, thoughtful, intelligent, and funny. She and I hit it off right away and had some heartfelt conversations. They had to work that week, so Norm and I went off to do our own thing.

It was May 2000 and we found that Nova Scotia and New Brunswick were not yet open for the season. We'd wanted to see the Anne Murray museum, the Hank Snow place, and variety of other spots, but they were closed until late May or early June.

We had both developed stinky colds but continued on through the day and ended up putting several hundred miles on the mini-van we rented.

The parts of Nova Scotia we saw featured rolling hills and shorter trees than we were used to. It was peaceful and rural. The people we met were friendly and helpful.

We visited several antique shops and gift stores, acquiring presents for our family at home.

Next time we visit, we'll call ahead to make sure they've flipped over their 'OPEN' sign.

Every few weeks, we go to visit my step-dad, DK. I've heard it said that the best thing a father can do for his children is to love their mother. My mother was deeply loved by this man. She met DK while she still had five kids at home. I was singing and on tour in Alaska. I finally had the chance to meet him on one of our visits home in the fall of 1970. They wed a few years later and were married for twenty-seven years before Mom passed.

DK is witty, funny, and a real partier. Mom needed that after years of duty and responsibility as a single mom. He took her on vacations and introduced her to the fun side of life. She was crazy about him.

Over the years, I learned to call him Dad. My feelings over the last year have deepened as we've helped each other through the grief of losing my mom and his wife. Six months after mom passed from lung cancer, he battled testicular cancer with bravery and acceptance of his lot in life, not defeat or resignation. I think the world of him and will be eternally in his debt for the way he cared for my mother especially at her end-times.

Today, Dad said the sweetest thing he has ever said to me. I told him I had finished the first draft of this book. He said "Well, I'll just have to read it then."

I said, "You'd really like to read my book, Dad?"

He replied, "Anyone who has taken the time to write a book deserves a little encouragement. Of course, I'll read it." At fifty years of age, I finally had a Dad.

From 1988 until 1993 when we bought our first RV, Norm and I regularly did what we called 'RV step-aerobics'. On the weekends, we would haunt RV shows and dealerships. Then we purchased a little twenty-three foot Terry Taurus travel trailer. Now we could holiday in the comfort of our own tiny home. This was a real blessing for me as I was finding it increasingly difficult to get comfortable in bed due to joint and muscle aches and now I could make the bed up to my specifications.

We stayed at the Pacific Shores RV Park in Newport, Oregon several times, enjoying their ice cream socials, pancake breakfasts, bingo games, and karaoke nights. Then they changed the park into a coach resort and our little Terry didn't qualify anymore.

Last year we stayed at the Beverly Beach Government Campground. What an inspiring place. The lush green ferns and forest surrounded us. The ocean was only a few yards away, putting the taste of salt in the air. The ever-present cries of the gulls made me feel right at home.

Travelling in an RV opened up new possibilities to us. We visited Lake Louise, the Columbia Ice fields, and Mount Saint Helen's. We went to Kelowna to see our son and his wife, to Salmon Arm, where we visited with Sieg and Louise, and Chase, to be with my sister, Sasha. It's such a freeing concept to tow one's home. We could stop along the highway if one of us 'had to go'. We could fix lunch or a snack, as required. If we saw a particularly scenic view, we could pull over and have a cup of tea. I could stretch out on the icepacks when the pain got too bad. We could take our little Muttly with us anywhere. It has always proven to be more economical than staying at a motel and eating out.

The first year we RV'd, I set out to prove that I could cook or bake anything I wanted to in our little kitchen. Most RV's are short on counter space but ours had eight feet of it. I prepared spaghetti from scratch and baked buns to go with it. I baked bread, biscuits, cookies and cakes. We roasted a ham and cooked up all manner of things, having guests for dinner as we travelled from one loved one's home-town to another. We often talked about 'full-timing'... just hitting the road and making a living with writing, photography, painting, and looking after campgrounds.

At last, we made a decision to 'Just Do It'. As we were preparing ourselves, I wrote this piece. It was printed as a centre spread complete with my colour photos in a magazine called Camping Canada, in December 1998.

"A place for everything and everything in its place." We are downsiz-ing from a seventy by fourteen foot mobile home to a 1993, thirty-four by eight foot (plus forty-eight square feet for the slide-outs) Canadian made Corsair RV. All around me I see piles of neatly priced and inventoried items... one man's junk... blocking the view to our future. There'll be no more wasted space. Each thing I look at in our home is now mentally kept, priced for a yard sale, given to someone specific, given to charity, or left out for the trash man. Lord, save us from storage, although it does have one hundred and twenty-eight cubic feet of outside storage. This totals three hundred and fifty-two square feet.

In past moves, it has all come along with us; in drawers that were just moved and never packed-up or disturbed in any way; in boxes that were never unpacked (I didn't know we still had every single pamphlet on every single place we'd ever been). We're heading into our second yard sale. It's odd to think that so much stuff means so little to me now. It's just been filling up space and that's really sad. It could have made someone else's life a little easier. We could have sold our kitchen table and six chairs about five times over by now.

"I'm not selling my Richard Bach or Belva Plain books, ok?" I holler out from the hallway.

"No problem. I'm keeping this golf book, all right?"

"Sure."

Our real treasures are now coming to light. We are honing, refining, defining, and being honest with each other and ourselves about what was meaningful in our lives. We've had to determine what is important to us, and what tugs at the old heartstrings. I'm starting to feel more liberated. I've got a clearer picture of myself, who I am, what I need, and what I value.

I spent an hour at our chosen home the other day. (It's not ours yet. We still have to sell our current home, all of our furniture.... the new deep freezer, the new eight foot dining room suite.... the piano (I'm keeping the keyboards)... and all of our other assorted and sundry possessions).

I took twenty pictures. I can now sit and place each of the items we are keeping in our new home. This smaller space will be as much a home as was our first three thousand square foot house. I sat on the chairs, I lay on the couch, I sat on the can, I lay on the bed, and I visualized us doing all that we do in comfort and with relative ease. There's a central vacuum cleaner and the least floor space I've ever had to clean. A cosmic joke, I'm sure.

We do have a lot of stuff that we want or need to bring. We both paint—he in watercolour and I in acrylic. We both use the computer every day for CADD (computer-aided drafting and design), creative writing, journaling, and photography. We both work from home; when my husband hasn't contracted himself out. I also play the guitar and keyboards, sing, have a little four-track recording studio and so on. We live a big, multi-dimensional life.

I have dissolved my salt and peppershaker, rock and shell, and angel collections. But I still do astrology and so those books have to be accounted for in the weight. We both enjoy photography and have quite a bit of equipment and lots of photo albums. Our walls are covered with pictures of our ancestors. We have a miniature poodle, named Muttly plus his belongings and kennel. Our music CD's and movie videos round out our daily life. But everything we bring will be weighed both physically and figuratively to keep us safe on the road.

The first three to five years we will live in Fort Langley, except for vacations, while we continue to work and save for retirement. We plan to travel and see our country of Canada. Then we will tour our neighbour to the south, the United States.

There have been some mental gymnastics in regards to timing. We have devised a plan. As I've said, we are going through everything with a keen eye to our chosen future. I have also made a list of all of the things we have for sale, and we have agreed together on a fair price. 'or best offer' always plays into times such as these. I'll keep an open mind. I hand out a flyer to everyone who comes to the yard sale asking them to please tell their relatives and friends that we will be having an open house and yard sale every two weeks until we move. When we do sell the house, we will then ask for sixty days before we move out. This gives us time to liquidate the remainder of our possessions, and make a deal on the rig we want. Timing can be quite tricky in these situations. All we can do is our best.

We are excited. We have wanted to full-time for five years. The kids are living their own lives and now it is time for us to live ours. We've researched parks in the area that take full-timers and found the one for us only half an hour away. It's right in the heart of the most artsy village around. We went camping there a few weeks ago and picked out a few sights in which we would like to live. We talked to some full-timers who answered our questions about snow removal, propane costs in the winter, and possible spring flooding. We picked the sites on high ground using the information from our future neighbours. They were kind enough to let us into their home to see how they set it up. It showed me just how homey it could be. They also advised us on who the partiers are and who enjoyed a more quiet life.

My questions and concerns allayed, we march together into our golden future. The dream will come true in due time. "God willin' and the creek don't run dry."

Well, we never received even one offer on our home. Then I got a full time position at a company in Burnaby. So, we have decided to forgo our adventure. As we went about our daily routines over the next few months, we realized that we live life 'too large' and wouldn't have been happy in such cramped quarters. Then, I was diagnosed with SLE (systemic lupus erythematosus) in 1998 by a rheumatologist named Dr. L. Jones. He gave me a bunch of answers to some of the health challenges in my life. Source works in mysterious ways. We have learned to not push the river.

During the first two years here in our house, we tried to sell it three times. We have never had a bite so I guess we are where we're meant to be.

After we made our decision to not go full-timing, our life made an about face. We built a gazebo and created a paradise for ourselves in the back garden. Seven months later, my first granddaughter we born. I'm glad we were here to support Darlene, and Burt, and to welcome Connie.

For my fiftieth birthday last year, Norm surprised me with a huge party in our back yard. Three-dozen people wished me well, that day. It was the best birthday I have ever had. He'd laid in a stone patio and a new fence. The flowers were blooming and the weather was mild.

Norm and I truly live a dream within this dream we call life. This place is a space we can go to rest our spirits and refill our senses. It is home.

HEALTH MATTERS

E veryone says how healthy I look. They also say, 'have you lost weight; you look so good.' Only recently have I found out how ill I really am. I have several health issues that I haven't been able to address in anecdotal form as the threads of pain and disruption of my daily life are so interwoven that it would seem like I was continually saying, 'and then I breathed' throughout the whole book. I have decided to simply include a note about each of them in this separate chapter.

Allergies

When we were on tour in Whitehorse, we lived in a big old house with the rest of the band. We all took turns preparing the evening meal. It was Sammy's turn to cook, and he was making chili. I asked what his recipe was and he told me. When he mentioned mushrooms, I said that I didn't like them and asked if he would please not include them this time. He agreed. I told him I had had some as a teenager and had been sick to my stomach. What did he do? He cut them into really tiny pieces and snuck them in anyway. Why do some people think they know better than the next person?

We ate our dinner and got ready to go to work. About an hour later, I started to vomit and was so ill that I had to be rushed to the hospital.

I couldn't stop vomiting and became dehydrated. I lost consciousness and they had to revive me. I was in the hospital for a few days and have never eaten mushrooms again.

When I was eight and living on London Street, a big furry bee stung me on the upper left arm. I went into anaphylactic shock and was taken to the hospital where I was found I was allergic to bee venom.

When I was seventeen a wasp stung me and I had a similar reaction only worse. I have a lesser reaction to spiders, mosquitoes, and earwigs. I now carry an EPI pen in case I am stung or bitten in the future. It is expensive but it gives me peace of mind.

In my mid-twenties, I tried lobster with my steak. My face went beet red and my throat started to constrict. I was found to be allergic to shellfish and have never had any since. The EPI pen I carry will help me if I am accidentally poisoned.

Last year (2001), I developed an allergy to cheddar cheese. During the month of January, I had cheese three times and each time, I became violently ill. I lost fifteen pounds in three weeks. The first time I got sick, I thought it could be the cheese. This was one of those intuitive thoughts that people can have from time to time. I then monitored my situation and found that cheddar cheese was the common factor.

I started to look at the possibility that I was lactose intolerant. I bought a product to help with that but I got sick again anyway. I then realized that the milk I put on the cereal every morning was probably what was causing me to run down the hall for the next hour. I stopped eating cereal with milk and the problem cleared up.

It's a strange situation because I can eat mozzarella cheese, have milk in my coffee and tea, eat ice cream and enjoy chocolate without fear of reaction. But if I eat cheddar cheese or drink plain 2% milk, I become ill.

I also have an allergy to radioactive iodine dye, which I found out about after being given some horse pills to take before a gall bladder exam in 1978. I went into anaphylactic shock and had to be resuscitated. I have several other lesser allergies to various odours, chlorine, wool, dust, and so on. These are not life threatening.

Dieting

I haven't really dieted much. I was always active enough with dancing, singing, working, and walking that I was able to maintain my weight for many years. I was always what I considered to be a middle-weight, but that was okay with me.

I'd weighed one hundred and eight pounds the first time I got married. Drinking and the resulting vomiting, not eating correctly, plus a very hectic lifestyle had kept my weight down. Even at that weight, I would wake up feeling 'fat' because my feelings of self-esteem were very low.

As my health declined and I wasn't able to be so physical, I started to gain weight. In 1991, I decided to follow a diet plan. I chose the "Fat Attack Plan". It was easy, straightforward and worked. Over the next eight months, I lost forty-five pounds.

This diet brought me down to one hundred and twenty-eight. I was ecstatic and became obsessed with my new body. I went on several shopping sprees and spent hundreds of dollars to clothe my new form. I went to the leather factory and found some short suede skirts that barely covered my, well, you know. After a few months, I started to attract some unwanted attention. This made me extremely uncomfortable. I'd always hid behind my size using the fat as a buffer.

I maintained my weight for over two years. In November 1993, I stopped smoking. Food became quite tasty and I began to fall away from my new eating habits. Then my health started to fail. The pain took over my life. I wasn't drinking or smoking so I used food as my distraction and coping mechanism.

I gained back all of the weight plus ten pounds. I maintained there for a year. Then I started working at a bakery. The first day, we had a taste test. It was for cheesecake. I had a small bite of each sample and made my determination. I resisted temptation for almost a year, maintaining my weight. Then my health got really bad and several people whom I loved died. My other bad habits weren't there anymore, so I turned to my original ally, food. I gained more weight.

Recently, I have begun to look at myself as a heavyweight. I don't like it so I have made up my mind to eat better. When I am well, I do exercise, take the stairs instead of the elevator, dance, walk, and do all manner of physical movements in order to bone up for the next attack on my body by one of these diseases.

I have discovered that I am not fat. I don't think of myself as fat like I did when I weighed one hundred and eight pounds and was drinking. My body may be carrying some extra fat around the middle. This is a challenge that something can be done about not a defect of character. My self-esteem is good today. That makes all the difference.

How I stopped smoking

In the fall of 1992, I heard from my sister, Victoria, that our mom had stopped smoking. This was remarkable. My mom had smoked for over thirty-five years. She was a chain smoker and I seldom saw her without a fag hanging out of her mouth.

"How did she do it?" I asked.

"She used a 'patch'" Victoria said.

"What the heck is that?" I queried.

Victoria told me what she knew about the new Nicoderm patch and I was intrigued. After our conversation, I called mom to see how it was going. She said not smoking wasn't troubling her.

My smoking had been troubling me. I couldn't do anything without a smoke. Norm had stopped fifteen months before and I felt really guilty when I smoked around him. This didn't stop me though. I was the type of smoker who crushed it out as I tucked my feet under the covers and lit one up as I sat up in bed in the morning. My lunch break consisted of three cigarettes over half an hour while sitting in my closed car. One time, when I came back in to work, a fellow co-worker shouted at me, "God, you stink. What is wrong with you? You shouldn't smoke." Everyone heard and I was absolutely mortified. If he were here today, I'd heartily thank him.

It was getting difficult to be able to smoke anywhere. We were a dying breed. I made all kinds of vows like 'I'm never going to Scotland because they don't allow smoking on the plane'. My life became very narrow and constricted.

I decided my time had come. I called the doctor and said, "I've decided to stop smoking. Please order me some patches and I will head to the drug store right now before I lose my nerve." He agreed and away I went.

I had a few packs left and I smoked as usual on the Sunday and Monday. I made up my mind that Tuesday was the day. Three smokes were left in the box. I knew that once I put that patch on, I wouldn't be able to smoke. I had the smokes before work. On my coffee break, I went into the bathroom to do the deed.

I was scared. I had smoked for twenty-nine years and I didn't know what I would be like without my cigarettes. But I was willing and that's the key ingredient to stopping any addictive behaviour. Determined, I slapped the patch on my arm and went back to my desk. At one o'clock, my supervisor said, "Aren't you going to take a break today?" Normally, I would have been out the door and 'smoking my face off' at twelve sharp. The patch was working for me. I ate my lunch at my desk and then went for a walk with a co-worker.

The next day, Wednesday November 11, 1992, was my first day without a cigarette since 1963 when I was twelve years old.

Two days later, as I left the office for the weekend, I felt as if I were walking a foot and a half above the ground. I was so grateful. I felt free. I felt like I could fly. It was another glorious gift from my Higher Power. I have never looked back. It will be ten years this November 11th since I have had to have a cigarette.

Hypoglycemia

http://guidelines.diabetes.ca/browse/chapter14

If I do not eat properly or eat on time, I become shaky, get clammy skin, and feel very ill. This means that my body is not receiving enough glucose to function normally. I can experience irritability, nervousness, anxiety, headaches, visual disturbances, faintness, and exhaustion. If I am unable to eat some sugar immediately, I will then lose consciousness and lapse into a coma. I could die. It is so important to me to keep my blood sugar levels under control. There's a lot of life left in me yet.

Some symptoms I've experienced plus others to be aware of:

- Slurred speech
- Headache
- Tingling lips
- Cold sweats

- Rapid heart beat
- Irritability
- Confusion
- Disorientation
- Weakness
- Hunger
- Faintness
- Dizziness
- Forgetfulness
- Crying spells
- Nervousness
- Tremors
- Coma

Author's Note: On August 13, 2004, I was diagnosed with type II diabetes. I am doing well on the medication.

Lupus SLE

https://www.lupuscanada.org/

For years, I have suffered from stiff and aching joints and muscles. I get a red rash on my hands, face and upper chest if I am exposed to the sun for too long. I will wake up in the morning with one or more purple bruises. They can be small or large and are in some interesting spots; most typically the inside of my forearms and biceps, upper inside of my thigh, or the inside of my ankle or wrists. During a flare, I may lose handfuls of hair. I might run a low-grade fever of 102 degrees Fahrenheit, have bleeding gums, and get daily headaches. The symptoms come and go at will and vary each time. I get tiny red and purple marks on my abdomen and the inside of my arms. My memory is sometimes short. I may feel exhausted. Sometimes I will also experience scleuritis–inflammation of the white area of the eyeball. I have also had vasculitis–inflammation of the blood vessels.

According to my rheumatologist, I have enough positive results to make a diagnosis for lupus. It is a process of eliminating other possible diseases and syndromes. I have since forgiven every doctor that has ever sent me away without a determination. It has to be as confusing for doctors as it is for patients.

Lupus is called the disease of a thousand faces. We all present differently. It usually begins slowly with new symptoms appearing over a period of several weeks, months or, at times, years. In general, as one symptom appears it tends to stay while, in turn, new symptoms develop. Because the symptoms may be hard to see or describe and tend to come and go suddenly, it may take time before the person becomes aware that something is wrong.

A little twist to this story is that I also have anti-phospholipid antibodies, anti-cardiolipin antibodies, and lupus anticoagulant in my blood and I am at risk for miscarriages. Anti-cardiolipin antibodies are associated with a tendency toward blood clotting. If this had been known when I was pregnant, I could have been given blood-thinning medications (aspirin with or without heparin) during my pregnancies to prevent the miscarriages. Earlier I mentioned that I'd lost four little boys. I might have gotten my six-pack after all. Oh, my gosh, five boys and a girl! Never mind... ☺

Until I was diagnosed with Antiphospholipid Syndrome a few years ago, I had always blamed my drinking for losing my babies. I carried a lot of guilt and shame about this. With the diagnosis came self-forgiveness and understanding.

Some symptoms I've experienced plus others to be aware of:

- Fatigue
- Unexplained rapid weight loss/gain
- Low-grade fever
- Slightly swollen glands
- Butterfly rash across my nose and cheeks
- Skin sensitivity to sunlight
- Scaly, raised rash
- Painless mouth/nose ulcers
- Arthritis

- Chest pain on breathing in
- Inflammation
- Rapid swelling of feet/legs
- Increased hair loss
- Vasculitis
- Scleuritis

- Headaches
- High blood pressure
- Blood abnormalities
- Seizures
- Psychosis
- Raynaud's phenomenon

Multiple Sclerosis

https://mssociety.ca/

I have been told by medical doctors, "OK, this symptom and that symptom are lupus but this other one is more like MS or at least something neuro." Too many doctors of various disciplines have had a look at me over the years. This comment is common to them all.

Over the years, my health has declined. I have terrible dizzy spells. Sometimes, my legs don't work and feel like jelly. Exhaustion can take over for days at a time and I am sometimes confined to the couch or the bed until my energy returns. More often, I keep putting one foot in front of the other and push my way through the day. Sometimes, I cannot. I go through periods of the 'dropsies' where I can't hold onto anything. Tea will go flying through the air, as my arm jerks out of control. My speech may become slurred. My mind may become dull and slow. My doctor thought it could be MS. He made an appointment for me to see a neurologist. As usual, the symptoms cleared up just in time for my appointment that had been booked six months earlier.

The neurologist booked an MRI. This time, the wait was four months. The day I took the bus out to UBC, I was feeling like death warmed over. The cold wind and rain on my face had caused a trigeminal neuralgia attack. I was in agony by the time I reach the University.

When I realized I was being put in a metal tube that was only inches from my face, I knew I would have to bring to bear all of my inner strength and courage. I am very claustrophobic. I had to wait an hour as they were backed up. I used it to good purpose, took a quarter tab of carbamazepine for the TN, and started to meditate.

I climbed onto the table and they strapped my head down. I closed my eyes and vowed to not open them while I was in the tube, as I knew this would cause me to totally freak out.

The noise of the clicking was extremely loud and distracting to my deep breathing. I persisted because I wanted the best test results I could get. I was not going through this again. If memory serves, I was in there for forty-five to sixty minutes. I was proud of myself that I had been able to maintain my cool and not show any weakness. This has always been important to me.

A few weeks later, I went back out to UBC for the results. There were only eight lesions in the periventricular white matter so no positive diagnosis for MS. I had an AVM (arterio venous malformation), which is a tangle of blood vessels in the back lower left side of my brain (the cerebellum) that could be causing some problems. Apparently, this is a rare deformity. Because my symptoms would come and go, it was difficult to treat me so nothing was done. It could still be MS but no one knew for sure.

I found this maddening and swore I would never go to the doctor again. I decided I would just accept what was happening to my body and live as good a life as I could under the conditions of the day. Every once in a while, though, I would get this desperate feeling and end up at my doctor's office. My thinking would go something like this... what if I'm 'bad' enough now that they will be able to offer a diagnosis and a treatment plan... what if a cure has been found... what if it is a slow-growing brain tumour that will now show up on an MRI or CAT scan and can be removed and I can live a normal life. That terrible thing, hope, would grow in me.

These kinds of thoughts would come every so often and drive me back to my doctor many times over the ensuing years. Through it all, Norm supported me in all ways. Our love deepened and strengthened. He would pick up the slack in our daily routine and cover for me. I had become unreliable, as it was impossible to predict how I would be on any given day. I would have to break plans because I was too ill to carry on. Sometimes, the only thing I would do all day would be show up at my job.

When we met, Norm and I could dance every dance and make love every night. Now, some days I had difficulty walking. Still our lives went forward. I'd found the man of my dreams and I was damn well going to enjoy him.

Like lupus, MS is another frustrating illness to diagnose. The symptoms vary from day to day within the same person and they vary from person to person. It's like a big Rubik's cube. When everything falls into place at a particular time and space, a positive diagnosis can be made. I have been told that I have probable MS. Then a few years later, I am told I have MS. More symptoms have been added during this last year.

Some symptoms I've experienced plus others to be aware of:

- Optic neuritis
- Nystagmus
- Fatigue
- Heaviness of arms/legs
- Tingling/pins and needles
- Poor coordination
- Spasticity
- Loss of balance
- Tremors
- Incontinence
- Sexual dysfunction
- Hearing loss/tinnitus
- Vertigo
- Facial pain/ trigeminal neuralgia
- Memory loss
- Difficulty concentrating
- Difficulty problem solving
- Slurred speech
- Burning/electric shock pain in arms and/or legs
- Burning on bottoms of feet
- Lhermitte's sign
- Babinsky sign

The stresses of 2001 started to take their toll in May when my daughter lost her baby. I hoped she wasn't going to have to go through what her dad and I did.

From then until December, when I went into remission, I experienced a variety of new physical symptoms as follows: blurred vision, double vision, excruciating pains in several spots on my body, inability to move my legs as they felt heavy and alien to my body, and the inability to feel certain areas on my legs and arms.

I started to keep notes, as it was so bizarre. Here are a few entries verbatim:

June 4-I experienced severe nausea, sweating, and felt like I was going to pass out, had excruciating pain on inside of left elbow that made me cry out. Balance of the day I felt tired, legs were wobbly, had trouble thinking.

June 7- I was sitting at my desk when I experienced a terrific pain in my baby and ring finger of my left hand. Area got very swollen and cold. Lasted for less than a minute then fingers had pins and needles. Ten minutes later, all is well. Happened twice more that day. When I went to bed hands and feet still tingling.

July 3-I was sitting at my desk when I suddenly felt like icy fire was running through my legs and arms. It felt like pins and needles, and electric shocks. The bottoms of my feet were burning. The pain was so bad that I couldn't concentrate. I left the office early and went to see my doctor. His partner was on shift and prescribed percocet demi, which did little to relieve the pain. He told me to get my doctor to check me out for MS as it sounded like paraesthesia. Over the next eleven days, the attack gradually subsided.

July 13-we'd gone to the mall. Part way through the first store, my legs gave out. They were tight and very painful. It was like trying to move through hot porridge. I felt exasperated and exhausted. I was scared. We had to get my medic alert bracelet fixed so Norm went to get a wheel chair and we accomplished our task. I spent the next few days on the couch.

July 15-we had gone grocery shopping and were standing looking at some candles when I suddenly heard a whooshing sound in my left ear. I then tilted to the left and fell on the floor. The next thing I knew was I was sitting on an office chair over by the flowers. Norm said I'd been out of it for about fifteen minutes. I was tired and disoriented for the rest of that day and a few days afterward. My left leg was very weak, so I used my walking stick. He hadn't called an ambulance because he knows my stand–I don't ever want to be in the hospital again.

July 28-the same thing happened in our backyard while I was showing our daughter the bike we'd bought for Connie. As I was walking across the patio, I heard the same whooshing sound and I again tilted to the left and started to lose consciousness. Darlene caught me and hollered for Norm. I slept for the rest of that day and used my stick for the rest of the week.

Aug 4-Dad's seventieth birthday party. I found a chair and stayed put in it for the whole time. I took not one photo. Felt trembley, shakey, not well. Left early.

Aug 13, 14, 15-had felt ok Mon morning, so went into work. Came home twenty minutes later as I felt so ill. Had terrible vertigo. Barely able to walk around our home using the stick and the walls. Legs very weak. Keep tripping over air. Often dropping things. Went back to work on Thursday but was totally wiped out.

Aug 20-26-have been suffering from trigeminal neuralgia and double vision for a few weeks.

In the summer, I saw the rheumatologist for the lupus symptoms. He confirmed the diagnosis. There were some anomalies that he didn't feel related to the lupus, most notable, a tremor in my left hand and the nystagmus in both eyes, both vertical and horizontal. He asked if I'd ever been checked out for MS. I asked him to make a note of his findings in the letter he was sending to my GP.

I went to my GP and related the incident to him so he could make a note in my chart. I already had an appointment with a neurologist for a few weeks later.

I went to this neurologist and had the usual exam. Having been through this several times before, it was very familiar to me. He suggested another MRI and evoked potentials. When I left his office he said, "I'll see you next year." Thinking he was joking, I called him on it. He said, "It will be about a year. The evoked potentials won't be booked for about four months from now and the MRI is booking a year in advance." I couldn't believe it. I would have to wait another year. And even then, if I'm not having symptoms when the tests are administered, there may not be any evidence of disease. It was absolutely maddening.

Through the fall, I experienced little relief of these symptoms. In December, they gradually lifted and I started to feel much better. For several months, I had only minor problems such as tingling in my lower left arm for about three months, several flashes of trigeminal neuralgia, slurred speech, and balance issues while walking. I'm quite fine to drive but walking is sometimes difficult. I'm okay to sit at my computer most days and work, but anything ambulatory is a real challenge.

The evoked potentials were booked for the end of January (some four and a half months later). I was feeling fine by then. They were inconclusive.

The eighteenth of July 2002 found me quite exhausted, sleeping well past my normal six a.m. rise. I felt foggy-headed, like I was pushing, both mentally and physically, through thick cotton baton. My speech was slurred, and I just didn't feel like myself.

For the last few weeks, it has been very difficult to do my daily march. Then on August first, my lower legs began to feel like weights again. The bottoms of my feet were burning, my balance was completely askew, and mentally, I was quite out of it. This was the worst attack to date.

I awoke last Friday morning, unable to walk properly. The bottoms of my feet were pins and needles, and I couldn't raise my feet to take a step. My mobility had been reduced to a shuffle. This lasted for over three days then gradually started to ease off. I felt like I had been forced to be on a stair master for weeks on end. My leg muscles felt knotted and really sore. I used heat and TENS to soothe the muscles. On Monday, I found it easier to get around, still using my stick. Today,

Tuesday, I am still quite sore but a lot more mobile. Now I need to work on smoothing out my leg muscles.

A new wrinkle has appeared. When I lean my head forward, I feel an electric shock-like pain shooting down my back. Oh joy, what now. I added it to the list.

The MRI is still three weeks away.

Whether or not I'm ever definitively diagnosed with MS is neither here nor there. I don't blame the doctors anymore. They must have scientific proof and positive results. The fact is, these are the symptoms I must manage alone, on a daily basis. We all do.

Trigeminal Neuralgia/Tic Douloureux

www.tnac.org

Trigeminal neuralgia (TN) is a disorder of facial pain. While the exact cause is unknown, it is thought that TN results from irritation of the trigeminal nerve. This irritation results from damage due to compression of the nerve from some source, perhaps a blood vessel. Or, in the case of MS, the wearing down of the mylen sheath around the nerves. It can be caused by the herpes simplex virus (from a cold sore).

The first symptoms of TN most commonly occur in persons over the age of fifty and affect women more often than men. For me, it showed up as a holy terror when I was twenty-four. The pain of TN is characterized by unilateral attacks that start abruptly and last for varying periods of time from minutes to hours to days, and weeks. Although mine began on the left side of my face, I now get it on either side. The pain quality is usually sharp, stabbing, cutting, tearing and burning. It has an electric shock-like character. The attacks can be initiated by stimuli such as light touch of the skin, chewing, washing my face, and brushing my teeth. It can also come about by the herpes simplex virus, which is lodged in the nerve. My husband, El, was always getting cold sores and he transmitted it to me through kissing.

Trigeminal Neuralgia is an extremely painful condition that involves the trigeminal nerve. This nerve has three branches that go to the eyes, scalp, nose, cheek, ear, the mouth, and jaw.

It is searing, jabbing and burning. It flashes for a second and is then gone only to repeat several times an hour for days at a stretch. It is unpredictable and debilitating. I cannot brush my hair or teeth. I can't sleep or eat. I can't have a breeze on my face. I can't talk and definitely can't sing. I am in just pain.

It is called the 'suicide disease' for a reason. Sometimes, I go out of my body and look down on myself screaming in the middle of the room and in a detached way I think, "I wonder if she's going to make it this time?"

I take Tegretol (also called carbamazepine) to give me some relief while the attack runs its course.

This ends my discourse on the dis-eases of Lynnie. I hope some of this has set your mind to rest or spurred you into action to do something for yourself, if you have a problem.

If you can relate to any of these scenarios, see your doctor immediately.

I repeat my 'disclaimer' here,

"No part of this book should be used in lieu of sound medical advice from a licenced physician. This is a personal memoir of my own experience and opinions."

AT MY MOTHER'S PASSING

The earthquake at 10:55a.m. on February 28, 2001 portended the fall of our Great Matriarch, Veronica Harris.

Feb 22, 2001-"Mom. Mom." I scream in a silent whisper. "Where are you going?"

Life-as fragile as a dewdrop gliding off a glass leaf.

"We've been together for only forty-nine years. I'm not ready yet. It's too soon for you to leave. Are you really done?"

You didn't know me tonight. You couldn't sit up on the couch and barely opened your eyes. We had all decided to talk about food to see if we could get you interested in eating again. Two weeks ago, I massaged your arms and hands. We laughed and joked around. You've been keeping a secret, Mom, your private life. That's ok. We're all entitled to our private life.

I talked to my sister Victoria just a few weeks ago to see if she would help me to call all of Mom's family and friends and ask them to visit, call, write, and/or pray as she had gone right down-hill. The doctor told Victoria that Mom was depressed, and she had been put on medication. We split the list, and before I went into the hospital for surgery, I had called my half. To their credit, each one of them made a contact of some sort. Little did we know that there would only be three weeks left in our mother's life.

All week long I've been crying and phoning and talking to Dad. He says you've had a little pudding. Victoria got some applesauce into you. If the cancer is gone and the x-rays are clear, why aren't you getting better? Only four months' time until my fiftieth birthday. I want you with me. Will you be there?

Feb 28, 2001-"All things work together for good." As I left the doctor's office, I saw some guy yelling at another driver. Road-rage. He was screaming at another driver, "What are you waiting for? Get moving. Do something." I took his message to heart. Instead of turning left to go home, I turned right and went to Victoria's office. When I walked in she said she was just trying to call me. She told me Mom had collapsed and been taken to the hospital by ambulance.

A few minutes later the doctor calls to say mom's O2 is low and her enzymes are too high. There won't be a CAT scan today to see if the cancer has gone to the brain. It is back and Mom's out of time. Victoria and I mobilized our forces. We set up camp at my house, she on one phone and me on my cell. Norman makes a pot of tea.

The calls are made, and we head to the Royal Columbian Hospital only to find Mom's been transferred to palliative care at Eagle Ridge Hospital across town. So, we drive to the other end of town, grateful that Norm is the one who has to handle the rush hour traffic down Clark Hill.

I look at your face and try to find you there. It's drawn and sunken. You were always so proud about wearing your teeth and lipstick and wigs. I look at your hands and recognition sets in. These are the type of hands I should have been born with; long slender fingers to glide over the piano keys. Not my short stubby ones (that managed anyway).

I leave the room and go outside to call Dad. I'm worried sick about him. You two are such a team; married twenty-seven years. He'll be fine eventually. But what he'll have to go through to get to that point will be horrendous. Dad answers the phone. I make a point of not crying out to him. He's already in shock. I know my mom's husband can't come to the hospital. It's too much for his spirit to handle. I say to him, "Thanks, Dad, for looking after our mom. You've brought her this far, and we can carry her the rest of the way. You and Joel look after each other now. I love you, Dad."

Eighteen people flood the room and spill into the hall. Norm and I, Victoria and Thomas, Catharine and Clementine, Claire and Vincent, Jordan and Muni, Joaquin holding baby Connie, Marilyn and Henry, Sandy and Wayne, Darlene and Burt, all take turns holding your hand and praying and crying and just loving you so much, Mom. You've always had a rowdy crowd around you. Six kids, eight grandkids, three great-grandkids, and nieces and nephews, and brothers, a sister, and a multitude of friends. We've come to say good-bye.

When everyone leaves, we go home. I try to sleep but it evades me. I cry, I blow, my eyes sting, and my heart aches. I get up to go pee. Please God, bless me with sleep. Please, bless my mom and dad and all who were there tonight. Grant us Peace. Dona Nobis Pacem.

Many prayers and tears later, I drift off.

I'm curled up inside you... floating in a bubble of bliss. ....ka thump, ka thump shoshhhhh shoshhhhhh bleep bleep gurgle............ muted sounds of safety, security, and serenity. I hear soft voices and music. I am peacefully at home.

PUSHED UNWILLING INTO THE LIGHT. My birth. PUSHED UNWILLING INTO THE LIGHT. Your death. Though it's almost impossible to think so now, we'll all go on, the circle, the cycle of life and death.

Mar 1, 2001-I awaken at 5:15 a.m. to find Norman on his way to work. I cuddle and cry with Muttly. Maybe some coffee would help. Might as well go into work early today. Now ready for work, I call the hospital. Mom has taken a turn for the worse. I call the office. They understand.

8:00 a.m.-Victoria is leaving as I arrive at the hospital. We hold each other and weep. We go back to mom's room and visit for another hour.

Her feet no longer touch the earth
Her breath's no longer strong
This woman here, who gave me birth
Will very soon be gone

Pending death changes how you look at things. Every hand movement and chest-fall is a triumph. What are those purple marks on your hands and arms?

You're still here so I still have a chance to tell you what you mean to me and say, "thank you".

Thank you, Mom, for your loving care throughout my life. Your friendship and support and acceptance have made a huge difference to me. Your thoughtfulness was amazing when you gave us the tin fish chimes for our tenth wedding anniversary. They make an angelic sound, and I tinkle them each day in honour of you. Every room in our house holds memories in the form of crocheted doilies, and crocheted dog-treat can, and afghan, and mug rugs, and photos, and angels, and pictures, and ornaments, all from you.

Thank you, Mom, for your genes, which made me love music, and rocks, and shells, and the ocean, and seagulls, and people, and good food, and the rain (it's pouring right now), and children.

Dad and Joel do make it in after all, around 10:30 a.m. They support each other. Neither is comfortable in a hospital. They have had a tough fifteen months since you were diagnosed on December 6, 1999 with lung cancer. They experienced your illness first hand and are both worn out. We cry together, and they leave shortly after they arrive.

I have vied for your attention all of my life. Being the eldest of five girls and one boy, it was rare that I'd have you all to myself. Though it may seem strange, I'm so grateful for this time alone with you. It is an honour to bring all of my spirituality to bear and try to help you have an easy passing. I say every prayer I've ever known, and some of the ones I've written myself. I sing you songs and read my poems to you. I keep everyone informed about how it's going. I write everything down, and photograph every detail. I know this is the end of your life on this side of the veil and I don't want to miss a thing. I've read all the books about death and dying for over thirty years. I want to be there for you. I have so many ideas and questions. I wish I could know everything about it, but I really wish we could go back a year and have none of this happening. I'm torn up inside. I pray some more.

Victoria comes back for lunch. Norm and I agree to meet at home at 3:30. Just before I leave, the doctor comes in. Dr. Morris is our family doctor and our friend. Mom's situation is hard on him, as well. Catharine and Claire come in for several hours. We talk and pray.

Norm and I go back after supper and stay till bedtime. On the way back to the hospital, I hear Amy Sky singing, "You're Everywhere". I break down again and fight to regain control before we reach the hospital.

Mar 2, 2001-Yesterday, we prayed and I told you it was okay to let go. But we all know how determined you are. It's what got you through your life. Was it a good life for you, Mom? We talked about it once. You said that Dad and us kids were all you ever wanted.

Victoria comes in before she goes to work. Today, I was thinking ahead. I packed up breakfast and a lunch so I don't have to leave.

Dad and Joel are in a cleaning frenzy. We all handle things in our own way. They can't come, and I can't leave. There is no judgment, only acceptance and support of each other's grief.

I grieve for Dad and Joel and the big hole in their hearts when you leave. They will have to come up with a new job description as caring for you has been their life for over a year. I grieve for Victoria who spoke to you every day and for Thomas who helped in any way he could to make your life better and for losing the 'Mom' you became to him. I grieve for Sasha, alone in Chase, crying in her rocking chair, knowing it will be soon and not knowing whether or not she should come down again. We had been told you could possibly go on like this for weeks. She was just down last week and is so glad she had a chance to say good-bye. She is recovering from back surgery and the trip is hard on her body but not as hard as your death will be on her heart.

I grieve for Catharine who has finally found and accepted herself the way she is. She is taking an entirely new direction but she finally seems so happy. I grieve for Claire who is so sick with diabetes and kidney stones but won't look after herself. This pain is much more brutal than those physical ailments. I grieve for myself. I talked to you almost every day. And we had a visit every other week. And I grieve for Norm and the loss of a 'Ma' who means so much to him. I grieve for all of your family and friends.

I know I disappointed you often. I also know that, in the end, you were proud of the woman I had become, a "Phenomenal Woman", you said. You could see how happy I was in my life. I think this gave you some peace, after all of those years of worry. Norm is the person for me. Finally, third time lucky? I'd made a good marriage with

Norm and peace with my kids and realized the profound joy of being a Grandma, myself. The first time Norm called you 'Ma', it thrilled me. We were truly a family.

Your breathing is shallow and rapid today. You're not waking up at all. You've lost more weight since last night. There is an unusual aroma about you. They put up a new IV bag today. The doctor says they usually only run it for the first twenty-four hours in this ward. It's been four days since you've had anything by mouth. I take the stick with the green sponge at the end and dip it in the water from time to time. Sometimes you suck on it, and sometimes you just turn your head. Is this an instinctive response or are you still here. I go with the idea that you are still present. You can go, Mom. We know you're tired. Don't let us keep you here.

When one of your girls comes, we cry and laugh and tell stories. We keep Sasha, up in Chase, posted throughout the day. We call Dad and Joel, too.

I've been taking pictures… because that's what I do. I've been writing volumes… because that's who I am. I remove your shocking pink head cover (it's so you!) and take another photo with all your stuffed animals around you. Your hair is grey and starting to come in again. Too late… it's all too late.

Victoria brought in a white bear. I brought in a little grey beanie elephant because you collect elephants. Teresa and Duff came in for a visit and Alistar brought a furry bear, and Clementine, a guardian Angel that I pinned to the pink ear of the elephant. There's another guardian Angel hanging on the bulletin board from Claire.

Surrounded by love just like always, Mom.

Victoria came back to have lunch with us. She will stay for a few hours while I go into work. It is period end, and the office needs me.

I don't want to leave you. Just like I have to eat and comb my hair, and brush my teeth and pay attention while I'm driving and hug Norm and our pooch, Muttly, I have to go to work. Life is going on all around us, and I'm still in the game. I wish you were, Mom.

It all seems surreal, like I'm floating, not really here but so vividly here. All my life, I've been told that I take things too seriously; I let things get to me; I should lighten up; get a grip. No one is saying that to me now and I'm grateful. But I have been conditioned to think this way about myself. So perhaps I am making more of this than there is. Maybe it's all a bad dream or I've over-stated it somehow. I really must have another look. Yes, you are on the bed with only hours or days left to your life here on earth. It's real, all right.

My mother is dying. Her hands, feet, and face are cool today. Not like the fever and flush from yesterday. Her skin is damp. Her feet, legs, hands, and arms are mottled purple and blue. Drool trickles from the right side of her mouth. Tears stream from her right eye. I put a Kleenex on the pillow and ask the nurse to turn the pillow over. She will be back to bathe Mom and change the bed. When this is being done, we respectfully leave the room, as Mom would have wanted.

Mom makes some guttural sounds every now and then, and claws at the bed sheets to get them away from her shoulders. So weak now. How can the sun be shining?

I look around to see if there's anything new in the room and spot evidence of Claire's nighttime visit… a love note, a small family photo, and more tearstains on the covers.

The nurses are attentive. They decide to turn her but she cannot tolerate lying on her left side. I don't know why. She pushes herself back against the pillows behind her again and again. I ask the nurse to put Mom back on her back. She seems more comfortable there;

less agitated. What difference do bedsores make at this stage of the game, anyway? But the nurses have a job to do, and they were very compassionate. We are grateful for so little interference from doctors and nurses... just enough to keep Mom comfortable. The Crossroads Hospice Workers are close by offering a listening ear, a shoulder to cry on, a yellow writing pad, and free hugs.

When I get back to the hospital, Catharine and Claire have come. The three of us have a loving visit. We all want to be with you, Mom. More tears and prayers and songs and laughter. The nurses are tolerant on this ward. We try to keep it within this tiny room but sometimes it spills out. We comfort each other and know the true meaning of being sisters. We're in this together.

Victoria says to read the pamphlet "When Death Is Near". I do. It seems the purple mottling of her hands and feet indicate her organs are shutting down.

All of my life I've thought about death. Do we survive it? "On Death and Dying", "Life After Death", "We Cannot Die", and shelves of other such titles fill my bookcase. Quite a few of my poems indicate that I am fully aware of my body's mortality and that I believe in the survival of the spirit. One of my poems "Cycles" says 'In crashing surf and seagulls fly, there's no such things as live or die'. I believe that. I think our body is just recycled back to the earth, and our Spirit goes on. In "The Master Plan" I write, 'But I will rise and walk away from this life so grand... To a better one, I'm told, that is the Master Plan'.

It's been a lifetime study for me. I don't know why. I only know that around the age of eight or nine, I became aware that I was going to die at some point. I've been preparing for it ever since. Before I leave my house (whether that's our home, our RV, a motel room, a room in someone else's house), I am scrupulously clean and so is my home. I am conscious of what I think, say, write or do. Often I think, *Is this the last thing I want to be saying, thinking, writing or doing?* I sometimes wonder what will be the last thing that I eat or say or do. I ensure that I tell everyone I love how I feel about him or her. I don't hold back.

Life is precious. People are priceless. Giving is essential to living a good life. Living a good life makes me happy. Being happy makes me feel expansive. When I feel that way, I realize how precious life is and how priceless people are and how much I want to give to them and how happy I am living this way. As you can see, it's a never-ending circle.

I am the family historian. I write things down so they don't get lost in the shuffle. I want to remember the facts and what was real. I photograph everything... from a casserole that looks particularly appetizing to my mother's passing. I keep the truth alive. Mind you, it's only my version of the truth because during the same event, our experience differs. In this way, our family is not any different from any other. It's interesting to note the unique slant each of us brings to our childhood stories. We all had the same Mom, but we each related to her in our own way. We all moved around a lot, and this impacted each of us differently. Our dad left all of us, and my take on this was unlike any of the other kids. The way that our mother's death would affect me will vary from my siblings. I write about my own truth.

You look so peaceful. I am bleary eyed; several nights with minimal sleep and a million tears. Don't they ever run out? Where do they come from, anyway? I feel as if a glacier melting inside of me.

I look at your chest to see if it's still going up and down. What will I do when it stops? I've never been in this world without you.

I'm a person who needs to be in control and doing my best to improve the situation. My mama is dying and there is nothing I can do. I can only be... be with her... a human be-ing.

We've all told her it's okay to go, that now she can meet Norm's mom and dad, Dorothy and Joseph, and Norm's sister Margaret, and Thomas's mom and dad and his brother. All of her family will be there to greet her... her mom, dad, sister, and brother, and her little boy, Darren John, who never made it, who never lived outside of her body.

I gave you a guided meditation yesterday... "You're a little girl, strong and healthy and running up a grassy hill. You roll on the green and smell the earth under it. The sun is warm on your smooth skin. You look up to see it. It's not the Sun but a very bright Light. You hear a bark and look down to see Taffy bounding towards you. She has a blue ball in her mouth. Her ears are flopping up and down. You reach down and pet her soft fur and find a leash in your hand. Taffy starts to lead you towards the Light. All of your family and friends come over the top of the hill. They are dressed in shining clothes of colours you've never seen before. They are waiting to welcome you. They will wait until you are ready. All you need to do is let go."

How could I be losing you so soon? I wanted us to become little old grey-haired ladies together, whistling at Pierce Brosnan. I'm forty-nine and you're only sixty-seven. Oh, my darling mother, my little sweetheart, I love you so. It's too soon. Thy Will Be Done.

Gluon-that strange substance that holds the Universe together. Mom-not quite as strange.

I remember seeing my friend, Foggy, in the hospital only a few months ago. Fifty-two years sober. He makes barely a bump under the covers. I look at him through the bars of the bed. Hazel eyes look back at me and he knows I'm there. Black goop is coughed up and spit out. I kiss him and tell him I love him and it's okay to go. A day later, I receive the call. My dear friend has passed. What's this death all about? Why do we need to die? I remember a movie I watched years ago, "Death Takes a Holiday". Sometimes, death is a blessing.

You struggle for every breath. The sheet moves up and down, ever so slightly. Your eyes are open and tracking. What are you seeing? I talk to you and say who I am and where you are and that the sun is shining and you have done a wonderful job and there's no need to hold on.

Yesterday your chest-falls were a victory. Today they are heartbreaking. You are trying to hold on so hard; fighting it; struggling with it; while I document it.

I don't want to forget this. I wonder who will sit with me at the end. I tell you it is an honour to be here.

I notice her left ear. My ears are shaped like hers—shell-shaped. I grab the camera so I won't forget this detail, and so I can tell a truthful story.

I see her slender fingers resting on the covers. I take a picture. I want to honour and remember every part of her. I thank her for giving me life. Life is a wonder. Now, I see, so is death. She gasps again. I wonder if it's a reflex. Her eyes stay open now.

The clock is ticking and I see it is 10:45 a.m. Moss covers the ground under the rhododendron bushes. They are bud-laden and will bloom during the next warm stretch of weather. But Mom won't see the spring of 2001 come in this year.

Norm comes at six for supper. He has brought fresh veggies, canned fruit, and warm chicken sandwiches. We go to the family room to eat. Each mouthful is a challenge. I want to be with Mom. The other kids need their private time, as well. Out of the thirty plus hours I have spent by her bedside, fourteen of these have been by myself. Alone together at the beginning and the end. Alpha and Omega. *I cherish all of these final hours with you, Mom.*

As soon as I'm done, I come back to your side. Each time I leave, I know it may be the last time I see you alive.

Is this alive?

I'm so grateful for so many things. We, your family of husband, son, and five daughters, all agree with and adhere to your wishes. We are all on the same side, yours. There is no squabbling or resistance to what is happening and what will be. There will not be any midnight miracle rescue. We help you to leave gently and go towards the Light.

It is discussed and thought that you might not be able to let go while we are all here. I want to be here when you pass, but not if it means you will suffer longer. Your kidneys have shut down and you won't survive more than a few more hours.

We say our goodbyes. We tell you we'll all be back at midnight after we've had a chance to shower and rest. I say, "Don't wait for us, Mom, if you have to go." We kiss you and leave at 8:30 p.m.

I put on my Amy Sky tape. She's singing "When Morning Comes… so don't say good-bye, just say good-night". I weep up and across and down the hill.

My mother is dying and still I must stop to pick up eggs, cheese, and milk. How odd.

I decide to set the alarm for two-thirty in the morning. I've heard that a lot of people die in the wee hours so if I'm there by three, I won't be too late to be with her. I am so tired. I'm vibrating, and my teeth are chattering. I'm freezing cold. Norm is worried about me.

I drift off. The phone rings. Victoria says, "Get Norm and come to the hospital. Mom doesn't look too good." We're there in fifteen minutes. I go up while Norm parks the car. Victoria is weeping in the doorway. "She's gone, Lynnie." She chokes out. "Our mama is gone." I hug her and rush into the room.

Mom's eyes are open and vacant. Her chest is not rising up and down. She's still warm. The covers are up to her chin. I kiss her and cry my heart out. My knees buckle; Norm is there, holding and soothing and comforting and alive. A chair slides under me and I collapse into it.

"Oh, my sweetheart, my darling mother, rest easy." I wail. Victoria and I hold on to each other.

More calls are made. Mom can stay in her room until we've all come to say good-bye.

Gathered together in grief and sorrow, we kiss you and pray and sing softly and wail and laugh and tell stories. I say a prayer. Claire sings "An Eagle When She Flies". We all say, "The Lord's Prayer". All life is happening now. From you, Mom, in death, down to Connie, your great-granddaughter, not yet two years old.

The chain is strong, each link forged solid and unbreakable. Norm and I, Victoria and Thomas, Catharine and Clementine, Claire and Vance, Jordan and Muni, Burt and Darlene and wee Connie bid you safe journey, mom. At four-twenty in the morning, we leave the hospital with Mom's belongings. We hug in the parking lot and say we'll meet at Dad and Joel's tomorrow.

Sleep evades me once again. Day four on four and a half hours of sleep, I'm amazed I'm still on my feet. At noon, we go out for a walk with Muttly. Halfway back, I collapse and weep in Norman's strong arms. I can't wait to see my family again. We are all in the same life raft together, just trying to survive this heart-wrenching blow. We know we'll make it to shore, we just don't know how. That's where FAITH comes in. Once again, I turn my will and my life over to my Higher Power.

After The Passing

March 3, 2001

The day after Mom passed over, it was decided we would all make sandwiches and meet over at Dad and Joel's. There was salmon, egg, and roast beef, a variety of pickles, and moist chocolate cake, which was so reminiscent of the ones Mom used to make and take with us to the beach or on a long drive. Later, someone else bought finger food and some drank a bottle of wine.

As usual, the house was full and the food was abundant. A good Wake was under way. There was music and laughter and photo taking and lots of good stories. Mom would have really enjoyed herself.

While we were joking around, I accidentally said the 'f' word and immediately said, "Sorry, Mom" only to realize that she wasn't there. These were the only tears shed at her wake, as far as I know. It was quite a shock, once again, to be reminded that she was really gone. I knew then it was going to be a tough row to hoe. Even given everything that had happened between us in life, we were close, very close. The whole family was as tight as a drum.

I don't mean that we lived in each other's pockets or anything like that. Sometimes, it was hard to get some of the sisters to call me back. What I mean goes way deeper than that. It was always that way with us. When we were together, we were tight. We are all completely different people. It is my belief that we became a part of the same family so that we could work on some issues that could only be resolved within this dynamic. I can hear my sisters now calling me a weirdo or something. I smile as I type this, because I know that I am a weirdo to them, but I don't care anymore. There's nothing wrong in being myself. Who else is going to do it?

After we ate and chatted for a while, Dad said we should all go in and look at Mom's jewellery. Some items had been written down, and her wishes were carried out. Then with deep reverence, we went through the rest of her treasures. We each choose some items for ourselves and for our children. Then, gathered around the table where we had so often enjoyed a meal together, we joined hands and gave a prayer of thanks and blessings to our mom for all of her pretty things.

Those first few days were strange. We had gotten close during Mom's end-days. Now we were drifting back to our daily lives, and it was another rent in the fabric of my life. I still felt 'floatie' and I cried a lot. Real life was playing out all around me. I was participating in it and enjoying it. But in the upper right quadrant of my mind's eye, I could still see Mom's body on the bed, yellow, her sheets drawn up to her chin.

There was an abstract concept running around the periphery of my mind. I couldn't quite get hold of it. Then, five days after Mom passed over, I got it. We were on the couch watching TV and suddenly it hit me. I sat up and explained this to Norm. I said, "The concept is–hollow. That's what struck me when I saw Mom's body." He said, "Yes, that's what I thought, too." Mom's spirit had left her body. It was now like an empty paper machete doll on the bed.

From this moment on, I have not looked at people the same way. Nor have I looked at death as I used to. I was always afraid of not really being dead but people thinking I was. I thought I would wake up in the crematorium or on the autopsy table or in a coffin in the ground. I know now that this is not the way it is and that people make sure you're dead before any of the above happens. So a lot of my fears surrounding death have been allayed. Death is only the end of the body.

The weekend after Mom passed, my husband took us out to Fort Langley in the RV in order to love some life back into me. We went antiquing on the Saturday. I was looking for a well-crafted jewellery box from the nineteen thirties or forties to put the exquisite period pieces I'd received from Mom's collection. We walked through the Antiques and Collectibles Mall. I found four candidates and choose one. But all the way through the store, I saw things that reminded me of Mom or that I wanted to buy for Mom or that I wanted to tell her about. I never knew my thinking was so tied up with my mom. I can see that she was seldom far from my thoughts throughout my life. We settled in early for a peaceful night at our favourite campground.

As if into a pile of leaf litter, my consciousness
dives to escape the onslaught of morning mourning memories.
deeper and deeper, under the covers, I dig in,
unwilling to realize the finality of your passing.

Mar 14, 2001-We all came together again for the Memorial. So much had happened in those few weeks. I had no idea that it took so much to plan a simple service such as the one we had for Mom. A few dozen people met down at the end of the pier in White Rock to say our last good-byes and then scatter her ashes. As the pipes bellowed "Amazing Grace", two flocks of pigeons flew between our heads. I heard the swoosh of bird wings and then someone cried out, "I felt a wing on my ear." A chill went through me. It was a twenty-one-bird salute.

Music had always been a part of our lives, and this day was no different. We had a portable music system set up. at the appropriate moments, specific songs were played in remembrance of Mom. "The Prayer", "Conte Partiro", and "An Eagle When She Flies". The writers read poems, which had been written from the heart... "The

Master Plan" and "I Thank God For You". Sasha, who most resembled Mom, gave the eulogy "Let's Remember the Laughter", which I wrote. Fall-coloured mums, collected by Victoria, were passed out to toss on the Pacific Ocean. Mom had been born in land-locked Kildonan, Manitoba but grew up by the ocean in Cordova Bay. She loved everything about it and was a strong swimmer. It was fitting that she was once again back in the Pacific Ocean. We all collaborated and contributed our part to the ceremony. Mom would have been proud of each of us.

"The Master Plan"

One day my heart will be quite still,
no blood will pump around.
And all the cells that make my body
will be laid in the ground.

But I will rise and walk away
from this life, so grand.
To a better one, I'm told.
that is the Master Plan.

I do not know the time of day
that this will all take place.
But in the meantime, I will pray
to be filled with His Grace.

I will be open to the voice
that echoes in my ear.
I'll trod the path of righteous choice,
and keep my loved ones near.

So, when my days are counted up
in numbers, great or small,
I will rejoice. I had the privilege
to live them, one and all.

Laughter relieves tension, and we were not without some humour on this day. Joel volunteered to scatter the ashes. Victoria placed the urn, which contained them, in a brown paper bag. As Andrea Bocelli sang his heartfelt song, a signal was given to Joel that now was the moment. He carefully retrieved the urn from the brown paper bag and opened it. I think we were all expecting that the ashes would be free within the urn. Instead, they were in a tough plastic bag and no one had scissors or a knife. Joel struggled to cut into it with his fingers but to no avail. My husband stepped forward with a key to slice the bag. This worked well enough. As he did this, I said "Mom always was the stubborn one. Now we can't even get her out of the bag!" Everyone cracked up and the laughter soared up to heaven to meet Mom and send her on her way.

"Burial"

her feet no longer touch the ground
her heart does not beat pound pound pound
her ashes scattered on the water
she tells me I am still her daughter
how could this be, her spirit roams
though dust of her is on the foam

"Seagull"

The sun cast diamonds on the surface of the water as the seagulls dove for them. One pure white seagull came in from the left, sat on a pylon, and watched us during the whole ceremony. She flew off across our site line when Mom's ashes were scattered. With a loud squawk, she disappeared into the blue expanse of the sky.

March 16, 2001
"Listen"

Yesterday, I cried and cried, like a little lost child.
I thought my throat was going to fall out.
In vivid living colour, clear salty water slid off my face and
soaked my pillow and clothes and floor and tissues.
She was never coming back.
My mom was gone.
The grief came in waves, cold and pain-filled
for if I had to swallow it whole
I would turn to stone.
There would be no tears
or memories
A hardness would form around my spirit
and separate me further from those who are still here whom I love.
In between sobs, I work, I play, I pray, I romp,
I laugh, I eat, and buy eggs, cheese, and milk
at the corner store.
Today, I'm tearing-up some.
There is a physical pain behind my breastbone.
My heart hurts.

Work is sometimes a wonderful panacea.

So is writing.

I can't feel her around me.

I thought I would

Maybe, one day I will, when I can calm down and listen.

April 7, 2001
"New Memories"

They call the veil that separates us 'Death'. I miss the sound of your voice, your laugh, and your quirky sense of humour. I long for your hug, and to hear you say, "I love you, Lyn." Though it's been five weeks since your passing, I still weep almost daily. But the tears clean my eyes and refresh my heart. The 'veil', I find, is thin. There is so much life going on around me. And you are so much a part of it. Things are blooming and blossoming, full of colour. Like the orange tulips that were at the first writers' group meeting that I went to after you passed, and that Jacquie gave to me.

I saw the orange (your favourite colour) 1951 (my year of birth) Chevrolet that sat beside me at a stoplight, long enough for me to take a picture.

And the cloudbank at the bottom of the hill that hid a twenty-one-story building from view. I knew the structure was there, I just couldn't see it.

And the movie that was shooting in our Mobile Home Park two days after you passed. All life is a stage, and we are but the actors playing our part. (to paraphrase Shakespeare)

And the elephant (you collected them) that trumpeted and stopped me dead in my tracks as I walked into my friend's office. It was a new jungle screensaver just recently purchased.

Our Christmas cactus, which we have had for seven years and has only ever bloomed in November, now has a single pink bloom. This is March and is the resting month of Christmas cactus'. That bloom is right where I stuck in a pink butterfly on a metal stick, which was originally in the hydrangea given to me by a friend when you passed. The bloom looks like a pink and white angel suspended and free-floating. It has lasted for three weeks and is only now fading.

New things to remind me of you. Special events are still happening between us. We are still creating happy memories.

I'll always remember the days gone by, of tomato soup cake with vanilla icing, and chicken noodle soup in a big mug, and warm crunchy monkey fingers to dunk in, and sitting by the wood stove, and doing laundry in the wringer washer, and singing around the campfire, and making up songs and poems for you, and getting the other kids to go along with me and sing for you, and long drives and even longer talks. All these things I will hold in my heart.

You still make me laugh. I told you I would listen for you, Mom. I have. But aren't you the clever one.

May 17, 2001
"Midnight"

I wear
Midnight blue for you
The colour of the night
The time of your flight

I wear
Midnight blue for you
The colour of the sky
The time of my great cry

I wear
Midnight blue for you
And for me too

May 19, 2001
"The Bulb"

We are as a bulb planted in the lily patch. It is in the ground and not visible to us. But it sends forth verdant foliage and flower to flourish in the sun and experience the rain, drought, bugs, loving hands, admirers, and those who don't even notice it and just walk on by, and sometimes walk on it, crushing it. At times, it is cut down too early. Until that time, the foliage is sending energy back to the bulb so that it can multiply and send forth many more robust flowers next year. In the end, it is all recycled back into the earth.

June 16, 2001
"My Credo"

I believe that I am a being of Light made manifest on earth by LOVE - the Source of All That Is.
I believe that my goal is to grow in Spirit and to help others to do the same.
I believe that the way to do that is by being a living example of peace and goodwill,
hope and cheer, calm and acceptance to one person at a time.
I believe that being surrounded by natural beauty enables me to feel naturally alluring. Phenomenal sights, sounds, and smells of the ocean, a flower, or the forest, refill my senses.
I feel refreshed and want to pass it on to others.

I believe that by making a special connection to each person I see, by smiling and looking them in the eye, makes a real difference in their lives as well as my own.

I believe in survival of the spirit.

I believe I will go back to the Source of All That Is for renewal and be sent back as a spiritual helper.

I believe in the goodness, gentleness, and faithfulness of the Universe.

I believe the Source sustains me and holds me firmly in the 'palm of its hand'.

And I believe all is as it should be.

Om

July 22, 2001

Death reminds us all that we are here as a single entity, connecting for a little while, then separating and continuing on our journey. As her spirit moves on, I can absorb my mother's life experience. I take into myself her determination, acceptance, and grace.

My friend Louise feels death is the ultimate out of body experience.

On an Oprah program I watched, it was Dr. Phil McGraw who uttered the words that have helped me the most through this tough time. "Grief is a process, not a destination." These seven words changed how I look at my situation.

My mom was no singer, and yet I miss her voice and the times she sang. I often hear her in my head singing one of her favourite songs to me, "Always" by Irving Berlin... I'll be loving you, always. With a love that's true, always... It's a comforting experience.

She was generous in her heart. Forgiveness seemed to come naturally to her. Practicality was the name of the game, and she was that. She had many notable qualities.

Because of her, I became generous in my heart. I learned to forgive my grandfather and my mother, who knew about him and invited him into our home anyway. She was no saint, and neither am I. She had her faults, and so do I. My mother became a human being in my eyes. When that happened, I knew I'd finally grown up.

Her death catapulted me into audacious chapter of my life. I became willing to take bigger risks. More often, I stepped outside of my comfort zone and did things that stretched me as a woman. I said, "Yes", to life and to going forward and creating my own way of being in the world. I switched careers again. I'd already gone from being a Mother/Singer to doing Credit & Collections. Now, I intend to do Energy Healing full time.

So, at the age of fifty, my life again changes course and I must go it alone without the one who knew me the longest and loved me the most. I'm hopeful that I will, at some point, turn this experience to good purpose. Everything happens for a reason in the wondrous design of the Universe. All I am required to do at any given moment is to show up, do my job, and be the best version of myself that I can be.

This is all my mom ever wanted for me and now I want it for myself.

SILVERGLADE

S even months after my mother died, I buried the best friend I've ever had. Louise Silver was convinced that death was another one of life's significant adventures ... the ultimate out-of-body experience. And so, I depict her final moments thusly ...

"She followed the same routine each day. Her livestock depended on that. Around six in the evening, she tied up her little dog, Yenta, on the porch. Then she went up to the coop to check on her beloved chickens. As she was leaving, she heard a familiar voice. This caused her to turn and look up. She saw the most wondrous sight she had ever seen and knew it was her time. She fell to the ground over the threshold of the door, and there she lay for her final sleep under a blanket of stars. A friend came for coffee the next morning and found her body. Her Spirit had left to continue its awesome journey. Arm in arm with her loved ones, she walked calmly into her future."

Grief is a process whose ultimate goal is acceptance of life on life's terms. This is what Louise taught me.

Most people never get the opportunity to experience anyone like Louise. I was lucky. For twenty-six years, her love warmed and uplifted me. It still does and always will.

I met Louise on a hot day in June 1974. She was stretched out on a blanket on the grass watching the kids in a three-legged race. It was Salmon Arm West's sports day. She shaded her eyes to look up at me as I was passing by. "You know," she said with that unusual drawl of hers, "I was born a hundred years too late. There is a caravan heading west out of Colorado and I would dearly love to be a part of that." Well, the writer in me was hooked. I was twenty-four years old and looking for some answers to life. My marriage was stalling, we were in counselling, my pill habit was taking hold of me, and I knew deep down that I was not living the life I was meant to live. I was scrambling to get some 'spirit' back into my life.

She was, at the very least, interesting. She said, "I know who you are. You're married to Elvin Saulson. My name is Louise Silver. Elvin and I teach together here. Have a seat. I've been looking forward to meeting you. Elvin has told me so much about you."

I learned she was facilitating a pottery class in September and I thought it would be a good opportunity to get to know her. I would learn something new and get out of the house all at the same time. I signed up on the spot.

That September, I went once a week out to Silverglade for lessons in how to make mud pies. I had no idea what it took to make a piece of pottery. I learned and found that I loved it. I was creating in a completely different way than I was used to.

There were four of us plus Louise. While we potted, we talked. We exchanged ideas. We listened to Louise's stories and parables. We not only learned how to 'pug clay balls', we learned how to let the air out of ourselves, too. There were no boundaries or no-nos. We were respectful and caring of each other.

Over the following twenty-six years I'd lived and/or visited there, it was always the same. Wisdom flowed both ways to the centre.

Sieg, her husband, was my silent dad. He was an example that I sorely needed in my life. He wanted nothing from me, only good things for me. Sieg was a good listener. He was a powerful presence sitting quietly, observing, and participating as required.

He showed me that a man could be trustworthy, respectful, and caring of a woman, something that I hadn't seen so far in my life. Only Sieg could look good glistening in the sun, wearing a red flannel underwear top, and sitting on his tractor. His lean body looked strong and able. Sieg the Protector.

Just after Norm and I purchased our RV, we decided to take a jaunt up to Salmon Arm. We were invited to park it in their yard. We turned right onto Kusisto Road off 50th NE, and took the first left up their driveway. I felt the backend starting to slip over the edge and I thought we were goners.

Sieg was on his tractor out in the field. He came and helped me out of the truck then pulled the RV up the drive. This was a really frightening experience for me. We were so glad he was able to rescue us. I was worried about how we would get back down to the road but it was not a problem.

He showed me that a person could be older and still be able to change. He stopped drinking without benefit of a support group. He went through treatment for throat cancer without complaint. He stopped smoking without the benefit of a patch. I was impressed. He showed me how to throw a pot on the wheel. I wasn't good at it as I had little time to practise. We laughed a lot while my wet clay object d'art wobbled down to a lump on the spinning table. I did manage to save a couple of short bowls with lids.

His pottery lamps, jugs, mugs, bowls, and pitchers were well-received. Every year they won the People's Choice Award. He would make the basic piece and Louise would decorate, glaze, and sometimes sculpt the outside of the pot. They were a well-oiled team. We own several treasured pieces of Silverglade Pottery and Sculpture.

During the last few years of his life, Sieg had to take daily medication for a particular health problem. This caused his heart rate to slow down dramatically. It is thought that he may have had a series of strokes because, overtime, the strength in his legs diminished to the point where he had to use a wheel chair. Then his memory started to fail.

The last time we saw him was in the fall of 1998. He was almost what one could call frail. I know he would have hated that term, if he had known. Louise and Norm had gone up to the shop to look at the latest project, get the sculpture we had purchased, and put it in the car. I sat at the piano playing, "Frauline", for Sieg. He clapped and asked for more. I loved this and sang some more.

Sieg died in January 1999. We missed him so much and Silverglade was never the same again.

When her soul-mate passed over, Louise grieved but didn't lie down and moan about it. She volunteered at the Art Gallery in Salmon Arm. She bought an RV and went on trips with Mona–to Bella Coola, and Gordie –to Colorado. That they never made their destination, due to mechanical problems, in one case, and a huge forest fire, in another, was of no matter. The trip was a huge adventure, as told by Louise. She got to meet Willie Nelson, one of her folk heroes. She was lonesome for Sieg but realized that her life was going, on and it was her responsibility to live it.

Louise often talked about time packages. Not everything lasts a lifetime so we need to appreciate these little interludes when someone or something is in our lives. Life lived at this level made more sense to me.

I understand now that some people are temporary support beams, some are short bridges from one thing to another, and some are there for a lifetime, becoming the structure of our lives.

When she passed over, I came to the realization that we had never watched a TV program together, or played cards or any other game, or gone shopping, or even for a walk. We talked. We listened. We ate. We created. We cried, and oh how we laughed. It was a relationship based on 'being' together rather than 'doing'. We enjoyed each other's company thoroughly. We never held back our feelings for each other. There are things that Louise told me that I have never shared with anyone else. We were friends.

Louise told me, "Always know when you are in enemy territory; walk softly, and quickly." This was good advice. I took it to mean that I should follow my instincts about people. Not everyone is good or has my best interests at heart.

She suffered tremendous losses in her life. She survived the earthquake in Seward, Alaska in 1964. Louise lost her home, all of her possessions including many personal historical and irreplaceable pieces, and her beloved dog to the Fly Hills fire in the early 1970s. She survived breast cancer in the 1980s. Three of her children, of various ages, predeceased her. That is a pain I hope I never have to withstand. My kids and I have our 'outs' but they are still here to fight and love another day. Sieg and Louise went through another fire. She endured the loss of her life-partner.

It was my habit to call Louise on Wednesday nights. A few years ago, she told me she had just finished, *The Bridges of Madison County*. I thought she meant the movie. She said she had been crying for several days and was finding it hard to stop. The flood of emotions that had not been released over the decades, had quite overcome her. This was a healing event for my good friend because it helped to open her up and heal a relationship that had been wounded.

On a whim, I bought and sent her the book. She got to page eighty-one before she passed at age eighty-one. Fate… I was given back the book by her son and have since loaned it to another friend.

Last March, just after my mom passed over, I called Louise on the Wednesday night as usual. There was no answer. I thought perhaps she had been invited out to dinner. I called the next night, and there was still no answer. I thought she was out feeding the chickens. I called the next morning and still nothing. I thought about it for a day because I knew my emotions were still raw, and I didn't want to over-react. Sunday night, I called the Shuswap Lake General Hospital and asked for Louise Silver. She said she would put me up to the third floor, and my heart sank. The nurse asked if I was a relative and without any hesitation I said, 'Yes, I'm her daughter.' She put me right through.

The first thing I said to Louise after finding out that she was okay was that I had told a lie. I mentioned that I had said I was her daughter so the nurse would put me through. She said, 'You are, dear heart. You are my heart-daughter.' There was never any doubt in my mind that she loved and appreciated me.

It is so hard to fathom what life is all about. With Sieg and Louise's passing, Silverglade has had to be dismantled. Other people, though they are nice, will be living in the old house and working in the pottery shop. Everything that Sieg and Louise worked so hard to build, is no more.

Or is it? What did they build? It was more that the pottery shop where you could go and create whatever you wanted at whatever level you were at and receive praise and encouragement. It was more than the vista view of Mount Ida to the East, the Shuswap Lake to the North, and the rolling pastures of other farms to the west. It was way more than the fire that roared down the hills from the south—twice, once burning them out completely, and the second time, just threatening them. It was more than the house that was more like a museum with its paintings and pottery and artifacts and glass insulators and baskets from New Guinea and Afghans that Sieg crocheted and Louise sewed together. It was more than the thousands of cups of coffee that were served at the hand-made dining room table. Sieg had made most of the furniture in the house. But, even at that, it was still more.

Silverglade was a sublime setting created by two remarkable people for the weary soul-travellers who came for nourishment of the Spirit. It was where you could heal from the wounds of the world—a place of peace, passion, patience, and perseverance. These two keep on giving through the people who were privileged enough to know them. Silverglade was a gift that was given from one heart to another.

WOMEN AND WORDS

On July 1, 2000, Norm and I, our kids, and granddaughter walked over to the park to enjoy the Canada Day celebrations. There were lots of exhibits and booths. I love to talk with people and was having a great time. As we walked up the path, I saw a booth that said 'Women and Words' (WW). I was intrigued.

I met a woman named Lucy who told me there was a meeting at one of the members' homes the following Saturday. That was July 8th, my forty-ninth birthday and I thought, "What a fun way to spend part of my day".

My twelve-step home group meets every Saturday at 10:00 a.m. and that was when the WW meeting started, too. It seemed I had a conflict of interest. I decided to go to my usual meeting and then join up with the ladies afterward as their meeting was going on until 1:00 p.m.

That morning, I was very excited. I felt a door might be opening for me in the area of writing. I didn't know any other writers and so I didn't know what to expect.

After my group meeting, I hopped in the car and drove over to Patty's apartment. I met Patty, Sheryl, Maggie, Lucy, and Alice. I felt right at home, as it was an informal gathering. They were very warm and accepting of me and of my poetry.

As the weeks went by, I gradually stopped going to my twelve-step group on WW days as I felt I wasn't giving either their proper due. I simply started going to the Sunday morning twelve-step group breakfast meeting instead.

My involvement deepened as I got to know and love these ladies at Women and Words. They became my 'heart sisters'.

That fall, I went to my first writers' conference and I have never looked back. I have plowed full steam ahead and entered contests and sent out submissions. I developed my own line of greeting cards, and then I put up a web site to sell my photos and books.

I write almost every day. I get up at 6:00 a.m. and write for an hour before my husband gets up and I have to go to work. I write for at least an hour when I get home. I write on the weekends and on my Wednesdays off. I write when we're away in the RV. I love to write.

A Power Greater Than Myself was with me that day in the park. Meeting Lucy proves once again that there are no accidents or coincidences in life. I just have to be awake enough to notice and say, "Let's go see!"

About Women and Words

Women and Words is a sisterhood of writers featuring most genres, ages, and levels of experience and production. There are no leaders. We work together to help each other grow, first as women, then as writers. We are self-supporting and contribute a little something to the pot each week. This is used to fund outings and lunches together.

Our group boasts writers in the following genres: science fiction, scriptwriting, children's books, erotica, non-fiction, fiction, poetry and prose, and personal/historic memoirs.

We meet every other Saturday at a member's house from 10:00 a.m. until 1:00 p.m. People may come and go throughout the meeting as their particular schedule permits.

The chairperson for that day will suggest a writing exercise, which we will do and then share with the group, should we choose. If we have written something on which we want a critique, we will bring enough copies for other members to put their notes on while we read the piece. We can also bring items that we are working on and read them without benefit of a critique. We share contest information, publishing ideas, and our book resources.

The meeting can swell from four to thirteen people with eight core members usually being present each time.

Life is life and that is what we write about. We share all facets of being a woman in these times… worry about our children and grandchildren and hope for their future; tears about an ailing or dying parent; concerns about employment; joys over publication; and the challenges we all face during the submission processes we are forced to endure to get our words out to the people.

Women and Words is a superb venue for any writer who wants support and acceptance. We are a uniquely varied group of people with big hearts and a caring spirits.

The Writers of Women and Words

We recently gave our first reading at a local coffee house. Just for fun, I have included the introductions here:

She is a writer with many facets. She can be playful as in "Golfers' Lament" or philosophical with writings such as "Soul Power" and "The Master Plan". Lyn opens her heart to the reader through her words, which reflect the experiences and passions of her life. Her works covers many genres from cookbooks to kids' books, with poetry and prose in between. Lyn's work is for sale on her website. Please welcome Lyn Ayre.

Though she seems quiet and soft-spoken, her poems pack a powerful punch as she champions for peace with her words. "September Rose" reminds us that the simple things in life can lead us to a peaceful heart. Her book "Removing the Sting" on living with Parkinson's disease, is insightful, joyful, and hopeful. Let's have a warm welcome for Patty.

Carolina enjoys writing science fiction and fantasy with a romantic twist. She wrote a script for Neon Rider, which was produced in 1994. Her prose is ripe with sensuality as she writes about such warm topics as 'Splash Kisses' 'Emerge', and 'Falling'. Her recent jaunts out into the arena of love are as refreshing as berry pie with whipped cream. Hello......Carolina.

Kinetic poet, Berry is energy plus. Being a mother of four doesn't tire her out, as you will soon see. Her physical expression of the deep emotional poems she writes, will excite you and charge up your batteries for a week. Put it together for Berry.

The "Story of Hector" is a delightful and heartwarming mix of humour and poignancy. One day a crow comes calling and stays for a while. His antics and intelligence add a new dimension to the life of his chosen companion–Paola. If you want descriptive prose that makes you feel like you're right there, then Paola is your writer. Let's welcome Paola.

These members were not able to make the reading but they surely do deserve an introduction:

Alice is a realist and it shows in her poetry. It doesn't matter where she is or what she is doing, there is always time to write a few lines and put a funny slant on an otherwise daunting situation.

Harriette brings out the kid in us all as she reads her children's stories. With a voice as smooth as caramel, she casts her magic spell. All are transfixed until we hear 'The End'.

Lucy is an intriguing political mystery writer. We are always interested to hear the next instalment of whatever book she is working on. She has moved away but is still an honorary member.

Lenora inspires our imagination with her poetic imagery. The antics of her story characters induce gales of laughter.

They're a tremendous group of gifted gals. My life wouldn't be the same without them.

2013 update: Women and Words folded in 2004 due to so many people moving or becoming too ill to attend. I've missed being with other writers.

In July 2013, I joined the Port Moody Writers' Group and have found an international group of sixteen men and women in this critique group. I love each and every one of them. The meetings are so helpful and I've become a better writer because of it. I've done several heavy edits of this book and feel it is more readable than ever.

PART TWO:

MADE WHOLE

PATH TO PEACE

Why do I believe in God? Simply put, because it works for me, and we don't do anything, repeat anything, that doesn't work for us. I've taken my life, which was fraught with pain, trials, and grief, and turned it to good. But how did I do this? I didn't do it on my own. I had lots of help. Until I surrendered and said, "I have a problem," there was nothing anyone could do for me. Even the pure divine being, The One God, underlying all of creation could not help me. It all had to start with surrender. Then came the willingness to improve myself.

Willingness is the key. I had the willingness to think it could be different if I just made one small change in myself, read the next self-help book, attended a seminar, listened to that inspirational speaker, changed my mind, called a friend, or helped another person.

Having faith means believing in something that you can't detect with your physical senses. Faith came when I was willing to surrender the notion that I was operating all alone in this gigantic universe, and that I had to do everything by myself.

During my life, I have experienced the full range of human emotions from ecstasy to murderous rage to piggish gluttony to heartbreaking grief to ruinous lust to humble service to paralyzing fear to inspired awe and everything in between. I'm just like you. I am a human being.

I had to learn to like being human. I had to leave my perfectionism in the past.

The gifts of these emotions have given me the willingness to do anything in order to be able to feel safe, secure, and emotionally balanced and achieve a level of serenity. What do I mean by anything? I mean I will make amends if I have wronged another. I will take the next right step even if I am afraid or feel it shouldn't have to be me all the time; the other person should step up, too. I will shut up and keep it to myself. I'll sleep on it. I'll do it differently. I'll look on the bright side. I'll let it heal. I will sit down and think about it. I will come up with a plan of action. I'll pray and meditate and ask for advice. I will pray for others who trouble me. I will stay focused on the task at hand and not live in the past or project into the future. I'll leave it at that. I will relinquish control to someone who can actually handle my life-God, as I understand that concept. One of my concepts of GOD is good orderly direction. I like that. It's a simple idea for a complicated gal.

I now have a deep appreciation for a loving and stable relationship. I know the balance that comes from saying, "NO", almost as often as I say, "YES". I feel the security of living a long time in one home. I sense the vastness of the Universe and my small part in it. If my life had been perfect, I wouldn't have been motivated to find some answers for me. Had I not encountered these 'pains, trials, and grief', what would have been the impetus for forward motion in my life?

I am becoming the person I've always wanted to be. I am content being with myself–in flux–in change. I don't have to fill every empty space with one of my addictions or with busy work. I am equally at ease being with others. I don't have anything to prove or promote or feel bad about, anymore. All of this has taken daily training. It didn't happen overnight. I worked my way through a few different programs. I'm still doing that. I'm still improving daily. Complacency is an enemy I recognize and immediately give the boot.

My thought life has cleaned up considerably. I recognize old patterns sooner and ask for help quicker. Then I deliberately move my thinking to another plane.

Things I think about sometimes come to pass, and quite quickly, too. Questions I pose are usually answered in a day or two. I believe it has always been this way. However, until I had shifted my perception, Source's gifts were lost on me.

Being in the moment; being here; writing these words; is exactly where I am supposed to be. Thankfully, it is also where I want to be.

While driving in to work, I may listen to the radio, to a speaker tape, or be with my own quiet thoughts. Today, I chose the latter. They led me to wonder, "How do I help others?" Since I want this to be the focus of my life, it's a probing question to pose. Throughout this day, I will be attuned to receiving an answer.

The answer came the next day. I serve others by immediately forgiving them their small transgressions each day, like cutting me off, failing to signal, not smiling back at me, not answering my phone call or email within a time period I judge to be reasonable. It is a decision that I need to make every day and Source provides me with ample daily practice. Be careful what you pray for.

Forgiving that small slight, overlooking that critical judgment, and not making them myself, is another way that I can serve and help others. By realizing that they are human, too, with struggles, defects, and gifts just like me, I can become a part of humanity as shoulder to shoulder we go on our daily march. Not everyone who speeds and cuts me off is a jerk. Perhaps they're trying to get to the hospital before their parent dies, or there's an emergency with one of their kids. Can I give them the benefit of the doubt and send them on their way with a prayer of goodwill for the day? What is better for me—to get angry and have those rotten chemicals circulating in my system or to send love and enjoy the benefits of the endorphins? Yes, it is about us and our reaction. They're gone and way down the road.

I am fortunate in that I go out to work only four days a week. I take Wednesdays off. For a few years, I spent this day in complete solitude. I'd sit at my computer and work all day, sometimes for twelve to fourteen hours. I did get lots of writing or photography done and I did create a whole line of digital products, which I now sell on my newly created website. But I didn't develop and nurture any of the relationships I had, or endeavor to create any new ones.

One of the gifts I received when Mom died was the realization that she was an extremely social person and always made a point of getting to know her neighbours and nurturing her relationships. I wanted to absorb this part of Mom into myself, so I made a decision to have a friend in for lunch every other Wednesday, and I've never looked back.

My higher Self has always put strong and loving women in my life like mom, both of my grandmas, Winnie Cooper, Isabella, Flora, Louise Silver, Maggie, Carol M. and many others. Even today, I am surrounded by shining examples like Bev, Pauline, Carmen, Halia, Ann, Chris, Laurie, and Brenda. As one passes away or passes out of my life somehow, another one comes in. I have never been without a shining example of faith and love in action.

A Soul is defined as core energy. It is my understanding that this energy underlies all of Creation. It cannot be destroyed only transformed. It is my belief that this part of our greater selves, our Soul, sends out a spirit that animates our bodies. Our spirit survives death.

I have an inner vision or a knowing that we are Beings of Light and Energy. I think this is why I have always been a Light-Chaser. Like a Raven, I love shiny things. I love rainbows, prisms, crystals, diamonds, disco balls, and anything else that will catch the light and reminds me of the true nature of my being. I have met and incorporated my baser side, and now I know I am a Child of the Light. But nothing I have ever done or learned has raised me above being a flawed human being.

This conscious mind of mine will never know the answers it seeks to the questions of the ages. The veil to the other side may be thin but it is not transparent. I am a seeker and so I pose these questions day after day. In a strange way, I envy Carol, Sieg, Foggy, Mom, and Louise's newfound knowledge. Now they *know*. I will *know* when my time comes.

This is what I do know now. They are not dead, as so many people understand 'dead' to be. Though their bodies have been reduced to ashes, their spirit is indestructible. This knowledge softens the grief I feel. It helps me to quiet myself, my heart, my tears, and really listen for that still small voice. I've heard it often, this past year. I now think of death as 'doesn't energize at this hertz', a bacronym I created in 2003.

As we were heading up the road to Sieg and Louise's house for the final time, we saw a deer on the pavement up ahead. Then another one appeared. I thought to myself *there goes Sieg. Oh, and there's Louise right behind him.* They looked right at us, then crossed the road side by side and disappeared into the bush. It was a strong feeling I experienced … a knowing that they were together and okay.

The next day when we mentioned it to one another, Norm said his perception was almost the same, word for word. This is often the way it is between us.

Oprah says that when someone we know dies, we then have an Angel that we know. I can't quite see Mom or Louise in shining white raiment. For Mom it would have to be a red gingham checked muumuu, and for Louise, definitely something purple.

My goal is to serve and bring harmony out of discord and wholeness out of fragments; first within my life, and then wherever I'm needed. That is what this book is all about. If my words can touch and help to heal one other person, it will have been worth the effort. If that person can say to themselves, "Hey, I'm not alone in the world.", then I've done my job. If they can see and say to themselves, "this woman has triumphed over the same situation that I am in, and this is how she did it", then I have served my purpose. I've done it through the sobriety steps, counselling, strong women and advisors in my life, different programs targeting specific issues ie: SeCure, and many others.

The word 'whole', in the title of my book, means being complete; having every part accounted for; being restored to full health. Our word 'healing' comes from this word 'whole'.

In writing this memoir, I am doing just that. My childhood was chaotic and completely out of my control. As an adult, I need to take responsibility for my life—my whole life. I can't change the facts of my past but I can change my perspective and perception.

Forgiving my past means that I am not wasting my life wishing things could have been any different than the way they were. I've cut myself loose from the bondage of the past. This way of thinking has brought me peace, contentment, and numerous other spiritual gifts. The reader will find his or her own treasures as their life unfolds.

As each memory is excavated, another one bubbles up. I go through some of the same feelings now as I did back then. The One who has

All Power transmutes them, fits them in to the puzzle of me, and makes me whole.

This is a meditation that I do regularly, 'There lives within me a little girl named, Lynnie. She is six years old; wears glasses, which she hates, and has auburn ringlets, which she loves. She has started school and is scared and excited all at the same time. I ask her to come and sit on my lap. Through my heart, I give her my undivided attention and all the love and affection she can take in. I give her peace. I ask her to be a part of me. I tell her that I value her. I recognize what an important role she has played in my life. She survived all of it in her own way, so I tell her I am grateful for that.' I am healing the child within me.

This last year has been a year of learning how to grieve and live my life at the same time. I'm getting quite adept at writing while crying, driving while crying, building a website while crying, writing books while crying, working while crying, and watching TV while crying. The only time I don't cry and do something else at the same time is when Norm and I make love. Then, we have such a good time that I laugh. As a couple, Norm and I laugh a lot. It's very healing.

I just have to let these emotions pass through me. Sometimes it overwhelms me if I think of it all at once. For instance, in this last year, I have lost my spiritual dad, Foggy, my mom, my Spiritual Mentor and my best friend, Louise. My daughter lost her baby last May. My sister is still in danger from a surgery she had in April, and my other sister's blood sugar is off the scope due to out-of-control diabetes. Also, her kidneys are producing stones, and she won't move herself to change her lifestyle and get a routine going. Another sister took 'the geographical cure' to Calgary after Mom died, and she just hates where she is living because she is so lonely being so far away from her family.

Norman and I found out we lost tens of thousands of dollars of our retirement savings last year because our financial advisor changed our risk profile and put us into high risk stocks without our knowledge or consent. We have no way to fight him as my husband is not working right now and funds are limited. My step-dad was diagnosed with cancer last week and has to have a radical surgery that might give him some more time. My doctor is retiring from his practice, so I have to start all over with someone new. My boss of three years quit and moved away; true, my new boss is nice but there again, I need to get used to her.

Is there any area of my life that has not been touched? Not that I can see. As I talk to people day by day, I find I am not the only one having a life-altering year. There is no chance for recovery from one incident before another incident is upon me. The layers keep building and sometimes I feel like I'm suffocating.

When I look at this paragraph, I have to laugh because it is ridiculous. It's too much for one person to handle alone. I wouldn't even think of handling it alone. I have a strong relationship with my Higher Power, a wondrous union with my husband, Norm, a network of friends, my twelve-step group, my Women and Words Group, and a variety of tools including prayer, meditation, willingness, surrender, hope and faith.

I watch Oprah almost every day and gain strength from her. I read inspirational books every day, such as 'The Twenty-four Hour a Day' book, 'Simple Abundance', 'The Prophet', and 'The Reflecting Pond'. I get caught up on world events once a month or so. Other than that, I do not read the paper or watch the news. I don't watch violent movies or shows. I try to keep myself on an even keel.

My tool of choice is 'FOCUS'. Towards the end of last year (2001), my friends were saying to me "Gee, I bet you'll be happy to see the end of this year!" It was like they were expecting something magical to happen on New Year's Eve to make all things new again. It sounded to me like the clock would be set back to zero and we could all start over. I thought this was a goofy way to look at things but I couldn't get this out of my mind. After a time, I realized I had lost my belief in magic. What if it could be that way? I decided to 'make it so'.

Since January 1, 2002, whenever my troubles, over which I have little or no control, crowd my mind, or cloud my thinking, I bring my attention back to the moment for this is the only place I have any power and that power is only over myself. I stay in the NOW – **n**otice **o**ur **w**hereabouts, (another bacronym of mine).

I allow the love that is in me for the person, with whom I am interacting, to flow out from me and wrap all around them. I allow the joy of being in a certain place or doing a certain thing, fill me up until I'm full to the 'smile line'. I relish any peace of mind I enjoy during the day; I let it soothe and heal me. I have heard many times, "It's not what happens to me as much as how I perceive it that makes me who I am." I do have a choice. Many times I could have chosen to slip into insanity. But I choose to stay here, in my right mind, such as it is. We all have a code. We have to do what's right for ourselves. And, this was right for me.

The last few years have offered me many opportunities for growth. I am learning about the human condition. I am developing a deeper compassion for others. I can still help others even when I am wounded myself. I've discovered whom I can turn to when I need a friend. I am learning that I am indeed a writer and writing is what saves my sanity. I have found that I am a spiritually strong person with a depth

I didn't know I possessed. I know now how deeply I can hurt and how fully I can love.

I see that crying, mourning, and grieving are healing, and that the decision I made when I was three, to never cry again, was not a good one for me. I've also learned that crying daily, just because, is not good for me as it sets up a chemical imbalance within my body. If I don't cry the first time, I won't have to keep crying throughout the day. So, I don't cry for nothing.

I do not tolerate self-pity in myself. I may get down for a few hours or maybe even a few days but I find it a total waste of time and counter-productive to what I want to accomplish in the time I have left. (As Morrie ["Tuesdays with Morrie"] says, "when you're in bed, you're dead", so get up and get moving, Lynnie.)

I do believe that we survive death, so this is a truth for me. Though part of what I wrote about Louise in the chapter called Silverglade was a dramatization, ie: walking off with Sieg. I feel it could have happened that way.

When mom died, I had Louise to comfort me. Now that Louise is gone, whom do I have? I have me, and mom and Louise and my old friend Carol M., just like always, if I choose to invoke the spirits and angels around me. I fully believe in angels and archangels and work with them every day.

I have Norm, in a new way. He has opened up emotionally this year. He has come to a new spiritual level. When I met him he said, "God who?" Now, fifteen years later, he prays and is forming his own beliefs. He is in the midst of his own spiritual awakening. He helps me. He comes to me with solid solutions like, "Try 'The Lord's Prayer'" or "Say 'The Serenity Prayer' and see if that works for you." or, "get to a meeting", "apply the art of forgiveness to this situation", and "let go and let God". Wow! He's not an alcoholic nor is he in the program.

What a grand day we had on Sunday October 14. Norm and I had made love the night before and I felt really good. The next day, I spent about six hours in the morning, writing. In the afternoon, we went to Barry and Lisa's so I could do a food shoot for Barry.

He is a Chef and had spent all morning cooking three entrees, two starters, a soup, a salad, and two desserts. Over the course of three hours, I took over two hundred photos. In between shots, we sat at my laptop and decided if we wanted to use it or how we could improve on it.

After a delicious meal, we returned to the computer to put together the words and photos for a brochure for his new business.

It was a day of writing and photography, high energy, and no pain, only friends and pets, good food and laughter. All of the elements combined to produce a perfect day for me.

We went to bed happy and tired. I got up at 4:15 a.m. to go pee. When I went back to sleep, I had the oddest dream.

…Norm and I were coming out from under some sort of huge tent structure, like the circus or a bedding plant area. I looked down and to my left and saw that the ground dropped off abruptly into a ravine. I thought, *Boy, I wouldn't want to fall down there.* But, that is exactly what I did. I lost my footing and slipped off the edge.

The grass was yellowing from the heat and patches of dirt could be seen between clumps of grass. Norm saw what had happened and immediately plunked down cross-legged on the ground above me. He produced a telephone book from somewhere and was trying to find someone to help me. He was doing his best. People were walking by me, and I could hear their thoughts, "Poor girl. Looks like she slipped and fell over the edge. What a shame. But there is nothing we can do for her now."

I was hanging on for dear life. I looked down and could see a culvert with water flowing through it. Then I saw three crocodiles swimming away from me. I was even more determined than ever to not let go and be prey to those beasts. I asked the Source for help and with all of my might, I hoisted myself up to safety.

Norm said, "Oh, good. You're okay. Well, then, let's just carry on, shall we." And with that, he took my hand and we walked on ...

The next morning, I did my prayers and meditation, as usual, and was struck by what I read in the *Twenty-four hours a day* book ... in part, it says, "The power released from within your self will change your outward life. I pray that the hidden power within me may be released. I pray that I may not imprison the spirit that is within me." Sometimes the answers come quickly, indeed.

In fifty years, my life has gone from Black and White to sixteen point seven million colours. Life has become faster, harder, heavier, deadlier, scarier, and with so many choices, it makes my head spin. So, I try to slow it down, lighten up, liven up, and focus my attention so I can be of more use to others and myself. I have a purpose in life that I didn't have a year ago. I have made many personal discoveries in the last year, as well. They are...

The show does not have to go on. I can take time to rest, live, love, laugh, and grieve.

I do not have to make a snap decision for everything. I can take time to mull it over and come up with a plan. "I'll get back to you on that."

If I do deserve a 'treat' it doesn't have to be cheesecake. It could be a book, nap, phone call, or many other things.

I don't have to accomplish it all today. I can say to myself, "Okay, good job. Let's just leave it at that for today." Then relax for a while. Go be with a friend.

If I keep all my 'options open' what will be accomplished? But if I make a decision, I begin to move forward and make my mark in life. Nothing can be achieved while I am sitting on a fence. And, I can always make another decision.

I have learned to not quit and run away just because one or two people are being brats.

I think world tragedies come to cleanse humanity by providing an outlet for unresolved grief. If you are already able to vent your grief, you won't find it as necessary to partake of the everyday gore in the newspapers and on TV.

World tragedies seem to consist of a group of spirits who decide to 'go out of this world' together for the common good of humanity. The decision is made at a soul-level, possibly before the people are even born. The group provides a vehicle for the world to come together in grief for a time, and then go back to their lives with renewed purpose to live their lives more fully by loving and helping others.

I sometimes think we haven't come very far from the Roman days of the Coliseum. With 'real TV' on every channel we don't even have to leave our homes to see people being torn apart both literally and physically by one thing or another.

I will learn much more if I don't set out to do everything perfectly every time.

I will be able to hear a person better if I listen then respond rather than react and start thinking about my comeback to what is being said.

I will be able to see what is right in front of me if I am willing to adjust my focus.

Worry and fear are just thoughts in my head. I can change my mind.

Life is about learning our lessons. We are doomed to dance the same poor dance over and over until we 'get it'.

When I drop my expectations, everything becomes a surprise and a gift. Source will always help me if I ask for it.

I have seen the Aurora Borealis twice in my life—once in Anchorage, Alaska while we were walking home from the bar our band was playing at; and the other time in Salmon Arm, BC (Notch Hill area), coming home from a gig we played in Armstrong—gigantic curtains of green and pink waved across the sky; it is a mighty sight to see. High-pitched ethereal tones shook me down to the soles of my feet. The experience filled me with longing and a desire to know about more universal things. It reminded me that the Source loves to dance, too.

SPIRIT PATH – A PERSONAL JOURNEY

T here are as many roads to believing and to living a Spirit-based life, as there are people who take them. What do I mean by Spirit-based? I mean keeping in touch with my feelings, intuition, and outside spiritual resources. For me, those are angels (Michael, Uriel, Raphael, etc.), guides (Mom, Louise, Carol, etc.), and masters (Jesus, Buddha, Quan Yin, etc.).

Each thought, individual action, and every intention I have ever held has led me to this moment. I have found it is the path, not the goal that is important. There is always another route–another way to go. I am never stuck if I just keep intuitively taking direction instead of focusing on the goal.

My journey has taken a twisted track. As a baby, I was baptized Anglican. I started attending Sunday school at the Salvation Army in New Westminster at eighteen months. A woman named Winnie Cooper picked us up each week for roughly eight years.

Then for two years, we went to the United Church across the street from our home in Ladner. At thirteen, I was put into foster care with an Anglican minister and his family. I was confirmed and received the sacrament of Holy Communion whenever it was offered. While in foster care, I attended AYPA–Anglican Young People's Association, and did studies in world religions.

I was astonished to learn so many other people in the world held vastly different views from me. I read the Bible, the Koran, and the Torah. I started to talk to people about their beliefs and experiences. I sought out people who were different from me and who knew more than me, so I could learn from them.

I began to delve into Spiritualism and psychic phenomena. I looked into UFO's and people from other planets and other dimensions. I guess I didn't think our own folks were strange enough.

At times, I'd experience the gift of knowing before something happened. I would sense it. This is called Claire-sentience or clear feeling.

When I was twenty-one, I had a near-death experience during the hysterectomy, which completely changed my view of things. Elizabeth Kuebler-Ross became my favourite author. I was also an avid reader of Jane Roberts and the Seth series, JZ Knight and Ramtha, Lazaris, Edgar Cayce books, and Richard Bach of "Jonathon Livingston Seagull" fame.

I've had good success with hands-on healing over the years. For example, when my son was little he had terrible pains in his legs, and when I touched his legs in a certain way with the intention of taking his pain, he would sleep through the night. Often people would ask me to put my hands on them when they were in pain.

I've detected charkas and auras, and done aura cleansings since the early 1970s. I can both see and feel the aura.

In the early 1980s, I went on a hands-on-healing weekend with my partner, at the time. I didn't understand or use what I learned, and I honestly can't remember much about it, except it cost my boyfriend about eight hundred US dollars for both of us for a two-day course. When I saw the word Reiki, it really resonated with me so I think it may have been Reiki, and I just wasn't ready for it. Having since studied Reiki, some twenty-two years later, what happened to me then doesn't even come close to what happened to me this time. Reiki has allowed me to spiritually heal and come home to myself.

Early in 1985, I began a two-year odyssey learning Huna, Hypnosis, and NLP (Neuro-linguistic Programming).

Then, for nine years, I studied Astrology with Donna from Pitt Meadows, Sandy from Surrey, and Brenda from Coquitlam. I've read rune stones, tarot cards, zena cards, and done numerology. I've worked with dowsing rods and pendulums (they don't work well for me), and I was a member of the Kabalarian Philosophy for a few years, even changing my name to Lorallyn Banner.

I've sat in healing circles and sent distant healing of various flavours, and taken many courses on the art of meditation.

Everything I've done and learned, all of the people I've met, the things I've given to others, those I've taken for myself, and the things I've left on the shelf have all helped me to become the person I am today.

As I've already written, for twenty-six years I was privileged to have Louise Silver as my Spiritual Mentor and Guide. She passed away September 2001. She is still with me and I can feel her comforting spirit around me. Over the years, she taught me many things about time packages; about how to 'protect' myself in the company of those who may not have my best interests at heart; about moving forward through the pains and sorrows of life; about gleaning every lesson to be learned from every experience I have; about the joy of love and laughter; about the sacredness of life; so many lessons; such a good example for me. I work with her now on the energetic level.

There are three very special women in my life – my mom, Louise, and my best friend, Carol–all crossed over. These women and I form a dynamic diamond when I do healing work. This just came to be one day. I can see the bands of white light joining us as an energetic team. I intuitively sense their energy, love, and guidance during the course of the session. Our relationship has shifted since they died, and I appreciate the help and advice they give more than ever before.

As an Usui Reiki Master/Teacher and Karuna Ki Reiki Master/Teacher, I have sessions with clients and teach all levels of Reiki. I also do sessions and courses in Aromatherapy, Chakras & Ch'i, Crystal & Colour Healing, Feng Shui, Life Coaching, Meditation & Peace, and EFT & meridian tapping, Reflexology, and Sound & Light Therapy.

In September 2003, it was my honour to teach the first course in meditation at night school in Coquitlam School District 43 at Centennial School. Up-coming, I will also have had the privilege of teaching the first meditation course at our local art centre—Place des Arts, also in Coquitlam. I've found my calling and my passion.

It is my belief that we are born with all of the value we will ever have. We have everything we need to be anything we want. We just need to awaken and remember then excavate and refine. This is what my life is all about—connecting others to their Inner Light and coaching them.

And so, on this path of coming to believe in the Source of All That Is, I find I'm like Dorothy from the Wizard of Oz who is told by the good witch, "You've always had the power, my dear."

AFTERWORD

E dward Morgan Forster , a prolific writer and seer of the future, urges us to not live in fragments rather connect so that we don't feel isolated.

That's the lesson for me in writing this book. I've been able to piece together my patchwork past. No longer do I feel confused or disoriented about my beginnings. I know from whom I have come and I know who is of me, in this world and beyond the veil.

It was quite enlightening to discover that my sisters' memories were just as fragmented as mine and sometimes more so. The process of writing unlocked the areas of my brain that were long ago blocked off or repressed. As one memory came to the surface, another one was hot on its heels. It was sometimes amazing to read what I had written. I feel grateful to be able to own and live in a whole me.

When I view the vista before me, whether it is the high peaks of the Coastal Mountain Range, the roll of the mighty Fraser River, or the plain of the fertile Fraser Valley, I sometimes wonder how it must have looked to my forbearers. What variety of poem or story ran through my great-grandma Elizabeth Cole Mackie Young's heart when she came upon it? Where was Great-Grandma and Grandpa Turner's house in Laurel, Ontario? With whom did my grandfathers work? Were they in love with their life partners as I am with Norm? Did they have horrible spats with their kids as I have had? Did forgiveness come after that, or was there a deep rift in the family? What was their human condition? Whatever their story was, I owe them all a debt of gratitude for paving the way for me.

Similarly, when I look out at the scene in front of me, I ponder what the world will be like for our grandkids: Ron, Connor, Andrew, Connie, Cynthia, and Logan. Focusing my eye past the cars, sky-trains, houses, and high-rises, I try to glimpse the future and consider the legacy I'm leaving for my coming generations. My legacy is my love, my story, and their history.

When I appreciate the intensity and world savviness of our eldest grandson, Ron, the financial wisdom of our second grandson, Connor, the true grit from our third grandson, Andrew, the dedication and determination of our eldest granddaughter, Connie, the vocal acuity and sounding of our second granddaughter, Cynthia, and the love and light pouring through our youngest grandson, Logan, I feel encouraged that our world will be left in good hands from this generation. These qualities and values have not been lost, though the daily news may lead us to believe this. I have hope for the future.

As my mind traces back along my soul-line from my great-great-great-great-grandparents to my great-great-great-grandparents to my great-great-grandparents to my grandparents to my parents to me to my kids to my grandkids, I realize that I have become a solid link in this chain.

The baton has been passed, and I have no choice but to run with it. It is my turn.

REMEMBRANCES

OK, you baby boomers, aging hippies, and middle-aged persons, how many of these things do you remember?

- Bathing in a galvanized tub by the woodstove
- Water heated in a black kettle with a wood fire under it
- Hanging clothes to dry on the line
- Standing the clothes against the wall to thaw
- Carrying out mattresses and pillows to the yard to sun in the springtime to disinfect
- Having the "croup" every winter
- Sleeping with all the windows and doors open during the sultry summer months and not being afraid of intruders
- Eating canned preserves and hot homemade biscuits for breakfast
- Putting the stewed fruit in a cheesecloth and hanging it in the fireplace to drip into jelly
- Warming your front side by the fireplace till it fried while your backside froze
- Vicks® VapoRub™ on your chest
- Coal oil in a spoonful of sugar for the croup
- Fear of having a tapeworm or pin worms

- Running around in bare feet
- Getting sick from eating dyed Easter eggs after we had "hid" them all day
- Getting the "green apple trots" from eating too many
- Jaw Breakers and Sour Gum Balls
- The hoola hoop and my mom being the best
- Swinging on a car tire for hours on end
- Playing *Twister* and laughing until tears roll down your face
- Eating Strawberry Candies, Banana Candies, and Licorice Cigars
- Making homemade wooden wagons
- Making homemade soup and dunking toasted monkey fingers into it
- Warming by a fire while you waited for your turn to sled down the snow covered obstacle course
- How good scratching your arm felt as the swelling went down from a honey-bee sting
- Those awful blisters on your heels in September from wearing shoes for the first time in three months
- Going to the outside toilet — even in snow, sleet, and hail
- Sitting on the porch swing
- Being scared from listening to ghost stories and haunting tales
- How about: *Kick the Can, Red Rover, Jacks, Gin Rummy, Canasta, Post office,* and *Spin the Bottle,* jumping rope, playing hopscotch, and shooting marbles
- Most people were baptized

- Fearing an atomic war
- Having buildings declared as fallout shelters
- Drills
- Duck tails, flat tops, crew cuts, page boys, pony tails, bouffant hairdos, neck scarves, bobby socks, penny loafers, saddle oxfords, poodle skirts, short sleeves rolled up, blue jeans rolled up, cigarettes tucked behind your ear, cigarettes rolled up in your shirt sleeves, Butch Wax, and Red Lucky Tiger hair oil
- '57 Chevy, drive in movies, hand jive, the White Spot Restaurant
- Banana splits and ham and cheese sandwiches at the Woolworth's Counter
- Remember how dark the nights were before streetlights?
- The fear of polio
- More gravel and dirt roads than brick or paved ones
- Sitting in the balcony at the Paramount Theatre
- Respecting our elders, especially our school principal and teachers
- Meals in school cafeteria were all made "from scratch"
- Pretending to be older by smoking
- Drinking Kool-Aid
- Your first coke
- Chocolate drops and hard candy at Christmastime
- Popcorn strings for the Christmas tree
- Dogs with rabies
- Fats Domino, Elvis, and the bop
- Cuban Missile crisis

- Assassinations and Vietnam
- Dancing the *Twist* and *Pony*
- High school consolidations
- The squeak of a wooden screened door
- Moth balls
- Making crepe paper flowers for May Day; and dancing the May Pole
- Not being afraid to pick up a hitchhiker
- Neatly patched kids' clothes
- The smell of bed sheets dried in the sun
- Straight chairs and no couches
- Half-gallon canning jars
- Walking on stilts
- Wood floors scrubbed with lye soap
- Sticky fly paper in a coil
- Pumpkins ripening on the ground
- Sears catalogue for 'at home window shopping' in the summer
- Sears catalogue for the outhouse in the winter
- Smell of fresh sawdust
- Picking out potatoes from fresh-dug soil
- Berry picking
- Shoe sole flopping as you walked
- Welfare day on the nineteenth of the month, which meant bananas, cookies, and chocolate milk
- Eating corn fritters fried on a wood cook stovetop

- The cold wood floor as you ran barefoot to dress beside the wood stove
- Cedar Christmas trees with colourful paper chains, popcorn strings, and bubble light

I can now look back on these memories and smile. I lived them all.

THIS BOOK WAS WRITTEN FOR

- People who want to know how to find and use a faith in a Power Greater Than Themselves to overcome and integrate a variety of life's traumatic events.
- People who are recovering or who want to recover from addictions, obsessions, and paralyzing fears.
- Survivors of rape, assault, and abuse.
- People who have battled the bulge.
- People who suffer from chronic conditions such as lupus, trigeminal neuralgia, hypoglycemia, multiple sclerosis, and diabetes.
- People whose partners have absconded with their kids.
- People who are grieving and are at a loss as to know how to deal with the death of their loved ones.
- People who want to live a life of passion, challenge, and peace.
- People just like us.

OTHER BOOKS WRITTEN BY LYN

For Kids

A Gift For Zachary

Feelings

What Can I Do?

For adults

One Woman's Journey

The Journey Continues

The Grateful Gourmet

Talks with My Higher Power

Humour I've Heard

At My Mother's Passing

Of This Space and Time

Little Book of Meditations

In The Light

Phrases & Fractals

Energy Healing Books

A Living Meditation

Relax~Release~Renew Meditation

Chakras & Ch'i

Activating Your Energy System

Crystal & Colour Healing Level One

Crystal & Colour Healing Level Two

A New Freedom: Hold Point Therapy and EFT

Create the Life You Really Want – booklet

Unleash Your Hidden Potential – booklet

Anatomy & Physiology for Holistic Studies

Aroma Basics

Laughing Buddha Herbal Course

Natural Perfumery: Aromatically Crafted Perfumes

Natural Perfumery: A Path to the Heart of Spirit

Natural Perfumery: Pyramid of Natural Olfactory Pleasures

Living Your Potential in the NOW

Make a Joyful Sound

Good Vibrations: healing with Tuning Forks

Bells of the Himalayas: healing with Tibetan Bowls

Heartbeat of the Earth: healing with native drums

Shamanic Journeying & Drumming

Spirit of a Holistic Business

Drumming & Journeying with Reiki

Reiki One for the Young

Reiki: the self-healing module

Karuna Ki Reiki

Usui Reiki Level One

Usui Reiki Level Two

Usui Reiki Level Three

ACKNOWLEDGEMENTS

I gratefully acknowledge all of the people with whom this book has become possible. I've heard it takes a village to raise a child. Likewise, it takes a community of family and friends to create a book. We, none of us, live in a vacuum. Everyone is interdependent on the other; a human chain of loving people stretched around the globe. We can do together what I cannot do alone.

I am especially beholden to my family, the writers of Women and Words, the writers of the Port Moody Writers' Group, our dear Eileen Kernaghan, my beta readers and reviewers for your support and encouragement. I appreciate you reading my book and offering your editing comments and critiques. All of you have played a vital part in its production and I thank you. Melanie Cossey, you are a wonder and have helped me so much, giving me a new understanding of many things in editing. Thanks to Erik, Robin, Anita, Gisela, Eileen, Connie, Farida, and Pauline for your insights.

I thank the original one hundred people who read my first draft sixteen years ago and gave me the edits and the confidence to go on with it. Your number one comment was, "Once I began reading your book, I just couldn't put it down. It helped me so much." I'm so happy you loved it and it helped you.

I'm grateful for the first purchasers of my book. So many of you told me you loved it so much you stayed up all night reading it. Many more people have bought it since then and have enjoyed the experience of reading my stories. For this, I am truly grateful.

FRONT COVER SYMBOLISM

There are twenty-one fragments. Some of them are fully there and some, barely there. Some are small and others, larger.

Twenty-one is a Fibonacci number. There are thirty-four letters in the title; another Fibonacci number. There are eight letters in my name, yet another Fibonacci number. I love Fibonacci numbers. From the first time I heard about them years ago, I've done my best to use them in my life, art, and writing to add energy to whatever I do.

The number twenty-one is a combination of the numbers two and one. The two is representing the dual nature I developed – one out in the Sun to please others; one deeply destroyed and crying out for help through an addictive nature. To heal, the number two seeks balance, reciprocal relationships, and selflessness. The one is reminiscent of new beginnings, independence, and opportunities.

The numbers two and one together equal three. Three is the number for my personal trinity of higher self, soul, and the Field of LOVE. The message for me is that I need to stay inspired, enthusiastic, and creative. There are three circles of self out of which the shards fly. They are my fundamental, physical, and emotional selves. The circles are a bit tattered but still basically intact.

The colour blue is indicative of a deep pool of water in which I bathe my wounds and from which I draw my breath. It soothes my spirit and nourishes my soul with serenity and continued trust in the process.

Yellow symbolizes inner courage, wisdom, and authority. I can use this colour to overcome addiction, confusion, and fear.

Red is the colour that a blacksmith watches for when forging steel. It means the rod is now malleable and can be shaped. Sometimes, I had to get this hot and bothered in order to have the energy to allow myself to let go and be moulded by life. There are eight red swatches to show this pain of continuous rebirth. I could say more but will leave it at that for today.

Printed in Canada